A God For This World

*Gospel Sermons For
Advent/Christmas/Epiphany
Cycle B*

Maurice A. Fetty

CSS Publishing Company, Inc., Lima, Ohio

A GOD FOR THIS WORLD

Copyright © 1999 by
CSS Publishing Company, Inc.
Lima, Ohio

Library of Congress Cataloging-in-Publication Data

Fetty, Maurice A., 1936-
    A God for this world : Gospel sermons for Advent/Christmas/Epiphany, Cycle B / Maurice A. Fetty
        p.   cm.
    ISBN 0-7880-1391-2 (alk. paper)
    1. Advent sermons. 2. Christmas sermons. 3. Epiphany season Sermons. 4. Bible. N.T. Gospels—Sermons. 5. Sermons, American. I. Title.
BV4254.5.F47   1999
252'.61—dc21   99-16011
                                                                                    CIP

This book is available in the following formats, listed by ISBN:
    0-7880-1391-2   Book
    0-7880-1392-0   Disk
    0-7880-1393-9   Sermon Prep

For more information about CSS Publishing Company resources, visit our website at www.csspub.com.

PRINTED IN U.S.A.

Table Of Contents

Preface

Throughout history, various religions and philosophies have attempted to save us *from* the world or have suggested we ignore the world or even deny its reality. Dualism, under several names, has suggested the world is a creation of a lesser god and, as a consequence, has little to do with the life of the spirit and mind.

But not Christianity. If on the one hand Jesus asked his disciples to deny the world, on the other hand he asked them to affirm it by becoming the light of the world and the salt of the earth. If on the one hand Jesus urged his followers not to be of the world, he did summon them to be in the world, praying "thy Kingdom come, thy will be done on earth, as it is in heaven.

In Advent, Christmas, and Epiphany, the Christian Faith especially celebrates a God who comes to us, a God for this world. God so loved the world that the world might not be condemned but saved, says John's Gospel.

God is not aloof or indifferent. He is not callous or uninvolved. Instead, God enters into our kind of world with all its brutality and war, with all its crime and corruption, with all its disease and heartache. It is God's world gone astray, and in Advent, Christmas, and Epiphany, we celebrate a loving God who comes to woo us back to himself. He is a God for this *world*.

Maurice A. Fetty

Watching And Waiting
For The Kingdom

Mark 13:24-37

The future is big business these days. Remember when in the 1960s Alvin Toffler came out with his best-selling book, *Future Shock*? People everywhere rushed out to buy it, from professors to corporate executives to housewives to investment counselors to ministers. Toffler told us the future was coming at us faster than we realized, so fast in fact, it would produce future shock much as a sudden immersion in a foreign culture produces culture shock. We become disoriented and unsure of what is real and lasting and important.

Toffler was not alone in his interest in the future. Universities devoted entire departments to studying the future. Corporations and governments developed think tanks to understand the future. Investment houses had their researchers sweating out their predictions of future trends as billions of investment dollars hung in the balance. In a less awesome way many weather forecasters predict our chances for rain for our lawns or lack thereof for our day at the beach.

If Toffler wrote one book on the future, hundreds wrote others. Naisbitt gave us *Megatrends* and Toffler came out with *The Third Wave*. Researchers and opinion polls intrigue us, but even more perhaps are we intrigued with the rise of astrology. Horoscopes are printed in daily newspapers. We all seem to know our astrological sign. Palmistry and various kinds of spiritualism seem popular. Edgar Cayce, an Indiana medium, was one of the most widely read authors of the 1970s.

Psychics like Jeane Dixon were published and widely read. Police departments unabashedly call in psychics to lead them to clues in unsolved crimes. The future is indeed big business. It's the key to success or failure in the stock market. As Will Rogers once advised, buy only those stocks that will go up. If they don't go up, don't buy them.

Of course the Bible is not without its interest in the future. The kings of the Old Testament often had prophets on the court payroll to advise them of the future. And generally the court prophets managed to say what the kings wanted to hear. However, there were exceptions like Isaiah, Amos, Micah, and Jeremiah. With a keen eye for world history and a sensitive soul attuned to the will of God, each passed the ultimate test for a prophet, namely, what he said would happen, actually did.

So much for the Old Testament times. How about the time of the New Testament? Were people then interested in the future? Indeed they were, especially Jesus' disciples. They believed he was God's Messiah to bring in the grand and glorious day of God's Kingdom. Even though the crucifixion smothered their hopes, the resurrection fanned the embers of their hopes into a high blaze. "Will you at this time restore the Kingdom?" they asked. And Jesus' disciples have been asking that question ever since.

I

When will the Kingdom come? Perhaps it never will, say some.

That is the answer of the materialists, the secularists, and the Marxists. We are well aware of the Marxist critique of religion as being the opiate of the people, drugging them into a vain hope for a kingdom yet to come, and delaying their earthly satisfactions for a never-never land of pie in the sky by and by. Karl Marx wanted to awaken people out of their false hopes and dreams so they would revolt and seize life for the here and now.

He rightly saw generations of peasants exploited and oppressed, often with the blessing of the churches, which sided with the aristocratic classes. He saw philosophers and poets and theologians thinking about the world, whereas he wanted to *change* the world. By worldly terms the kingdom had come for the plutocracy and aristocracy. The lord of the manor may have enjoyed an existence that had the appearances of paradise — a paradise made possible by the endless toil of the proletariat.

Therefore, Marx warned the masses that the kingdom of heaven of which the church spoke never would come. It was a hoax, a delusion, a device for keeping down the frustrations of the masses. "Wake up," said Marx. "Workers of the world unite. It is time for the proletarian revolution. The only kingdom is the kingdom we make for ourselves now. Therefore, let us be done with religious illusion. Let us throw off the yoke of serfdom. We have only one life. Let's live it now."

If we cast a critical eye at American advertising, we readily see that at least a part of the Marxist philosophy is deeply imbedded in our capitalist society. "We live only once," is the common phrase, or, "We go 'round only once." Might as well make it the best possible. Both Marxism and capitalism are basically materialistic in their philosophies. Both make every possible effort to "make it" in this life through the acquisition of as many things and experiences as possible, with the exception that capitalism is immensely more successful than Marxism. Nevertheless, a materialistic philosophy underlies them both.

Therefore, even in our culture it is not uncommon for one to hear people say that as far as they are concerned, the good life is probably it for them. They've lived in a good land with a good family with a fair amount of the world's goods. All in all, it's been a good life. And so they say, "If, when I lay me down to my final sleep, I never again awake, it is well. I have no complaints. Whatever kingdom there was to be, has already been."

II

However, as a church, we are here to say with the Church of the centuries that indeed the kingdom has come and is yet to come. It has already arrived, but it is not yet completed or consummated.

It is no secret that one of the biggest adjustments of the early Church was the delay of Christ's Second Coming. First generation Christians had been led to believe Jesus was coming again in great power and glory in their lifetime. If the powers of Judea and Rome had done him in the first time, Jesus would come again by the power of the resurrection and exaltation to put all nations under his feet, to subdue all principalities and powers, to subjugate all potentates and pretenders to power, to destroy even death itself. It was in this hope for glory that first century Christians were greatly disappointed. Consequently, the Church settled in for the long winter of its discontent.

And yet, it was not entirely a winter of discontent. For as John's Gospel and Paul's writings assured them, Christ had come to them again a second time by giving them his Spirit. It was a Spirit of rebirth, a Spirit of power and presence, a Spirit of guidance and assurance. Although the Kingdom of God had not come in its full power and glory, it *had* come, nevertheless, and it did have power and glory.

Don't look here or there for the kingdom, said Jesus, for the kingdom is within you. That is, the realities of the kingdom do not depend upon external acquisitions, but upon internal dispositions. The real kingdom, the real domain of the King is the human heart. God has all the material possessions he needs. What he longs for is the love and loyalty of the human heart and mind. When we swear allegiance to the King we belong to him, and there is a very real sense in which the Kingdom has come already.

Of course, this could sound like double-talk or illusion or another opiate of the people. But on the other hand it could be a tremendous release from the anxiety of compulsive materialism. If religion holds out the promise of pie in the sky by and by, doesn't materialism do so even more? Do we not all look forward to that day when we finally will have arrived? Think of it — that day when we can buy whatever our heart desires, when bills and breakdowns bother us not at all.

But doesn't materialism hold out the ever-elusive carrot? We look for the next bigger deal, the third condominium, the best ever vacation, the dream house about to be realized. If Marxism criticizes the Church for delayed gratification, think what materialistic capitalism does. Years of education, more years of training and working our way up, and then if our health holds out and we are lucky, we may get into the upper echelons of management or leadership. Delayed gratification? You bet. No wonder the '60s generation wanted to live now, not in some distant future that might never be.

But in its wait for the kingdom, the Church attempts to cut through both delusions, the Marxist and the capitalist, by saying ultimately God's Kingdom is not of this world. It says that powerfully by asking the haunting question, with Peggy Lee, if that's all there is when we reach the top of the heap, and discover the soul's emptiness. Isn't there something more for the soul of man?

The Church says it powerfully even amid the frantic materialism of this religious season by saying that a man's life does not consist in the abundance of his possessions, but in how he relates to God and to his wife and family and fellow-workers. The Church speaks it powerfully when amid the wild-war music raging largely over oil and territory, we sing "Silent Night, Holy Night" and "Joy To The World, The Lord Is Come" and when our choirs sing again and again Handel's immortal *Messiah.*

Yes, we are watching and waiting for the fullness of the Kingdom. No, we do not think the Jerry Falwells and Hal Lindseys know when that final day will be. Yes, we do believe God will consummate his great scheme for human history and that he has already begun by giving us the Spirit of his Risen Christ. Yes, we are released from the capitalist anxiety of having to live out a *New Yorker* advertisement in every detail. And yes, we are released from the anxiety of the Marxist dogma that we have to make it in this life or not make it at all. Oh, for the teeming, suffering oppressed masses of the world, there has to be a better day, a kingdom of God coming, when all is joy and peace for them as well.

We live between a Kingdom that has already begun, but is not yet completed; a Kingdom already activated, but not yet consummated. We gather around the table which focuses on a cross that inaugurated that Kingdom and which draws our attention to a living presence which some glad day, to the sound of trumpets and heavenly choirs, will bring that Kingdom into triumph. And so together we eat and drink in anticipation, proclaiming the Lord's death and resurrection until he comes again, feasting in hope for all humankind, that our loving Heavenly Father will bring all his children to that grand banquet feast, that marriage supper of the lamb, in the exquisite and everlasting joys of Heaven.

Prayer

Lord of the universe, who has filled the far reaches of space with galaxies and solar systems beyond numbering, but who in tenderness and affection has fashioned us in your image, we praise you for the marvel of the world and the life therein. In your mighty presence all the morning stars sing together for joy, but you bend your ear to hear the tiny baby's cry and to take note when even the sparrow falls. We come before you to celebrate your power and love.

And yet, O Lord, we come before you praising you not only for the glory of the world, but lamenting as well its grinding misery. The beauty of a thousand hills is counterbalanced by the ugliness of society's underbelly. The fame and glitter of the rich and successful are starkly contrasted by starving babies and emaciated mothers with no milk for their young. If a few in the world live in freedom and luxury, too many of us live in oppression and poverty. If many have tasted the delights of salvation and have known the grace and truth which come from our Lord Jesus, so many more have been without hope in this world and with no promise for the next.

So we pray earnestly for the coming of your kingdom, O Lord. As love and grace and truth have come to us through your Christ, so might his spirit of power and presence visit many more of the world's hopeless. As many of us have been liberated from human tyranny and torture, so might a new day of liberation come for the world's teeming masses yearning to breathe free. If some of us have known the joy of the earth's harvest and the exhilaration of success and wealth, so might many be brought to that glorious day of sharing fully in the world's abundance, singing the glad songs of union and victory around your table, your eternal banquet feast of love. In ways great or small, help us be instruments of your coming kingdom, O Lord. Through Jesus Christ our Lord. Amen.

How To Prepare For Christmas

Mark 1:1-8

To tell you the truth, it doesn't look much like Christmas at all. In fact, if you were to go there, you would have difficulty associating the scene with Advent or Christmas. It is stark, barren, very hot in summer and warm in winter, with no ice or snow. There would be no evidence of the reds and greens we associate with this season. Christmas trees would be absent, as would mistletoe.

Not only would it not look like Christmas, it would not sound like Christmas. Bing Crosby wouldn't be crooning through shopping mall loudspeakers in his silken 1950s voice that he was "dreaming of a white Christmas." Santa Claus, reindeer, and jingle bells would be as foreign to this place as space travel. And presents brightly wrapped and ribboned would not be found piled high beneath Christmas trees waiting for the uncontrolled Christmas morning glee of excited, wide-eyed children.

And this place wouldn't taste like Christmas either. You would find no boar's head festival, no partridge in a pear tree for roasting, and no plum pudding. There would be no cherry pie even for good boys, no turkey, no beef or ham or Christmas wine.

And yet this strange place was the setting for preparing for the first coming of the Christ. It is a place some have visited — a wild and desolate place eleven or twelve hundred feet below sea level, by the Jordan River, just north of Jericho, where John the Baptist was preaching. Poor John, attired in the rough camel's hair coat like that worn by prophets Elijah and Elisha nine centuries earlier, would be amazed at the Christmas finery displayed with abundance in our elegant clothing stores.

Poor John, living in caves in the wilderness of Judea and eating only roasted locusts and the honey from wild bees, would be astounded at our Christmas preparations of burgeoning supermarkets, sumptuous office parties, open houses, and holiday dinner parties of gourmet elegance.

And yet it is this famous John the Baptist, so poor, so alone, so disciplined and devoted, so piercing and powerful, who teaches us best how to prepare for Christmas. If nearly twenty centuries ago he worked to prepare his people to receive the coming Christ, so too in these latter days he would help make us ready to receive the Christ anew.

And what is his advice? It is ever old and ever new. We are to confess our sins, repent, and get ready for judgment.

I

Let us consider first the matter of *judgment*.

This word "judgment" does not sit well with us today. We are not sympathetic toward those who are critical and judgmental toward us. If we sense they are judging us, we quickly look for ways to judge them. If they are ready always to point out our faults, we are just as ready to point out their faults.

If the idea of judgment does not sit well with respect to other people, neither does it sit well with respect to God. We have come to believe in a God who is kindly, tolerant, benevolent, and just a regular, nice guy. He's sort of like a personal valet who jumps up to help us with our problems, but who discreetly waits on the sidelines when we are able to do our own thing. Although our God is not senile, he is conveniently forgetful of any of our wrongdoings. And we are confident God will, as one writer puts it, "always forgive because it is his business to forgive."

But not without true judgment, thunders John the Baptist to the crowds assembled to hear him in the Jordan River valley. Drawing on autumn-harvest metaphors, John affirms that God sifts the good from the bad and burns the bad with unquenchable fire, just as the farmer burns the bad chaff separated from the good wheat. And once the fields are harvested and set ablaze to flush out the snakes and rats, so God's judgment fires will flush out the snakes and rats hiding in the holes and crevices of human society. You prepare for the coming Christ by accepting God's judgment, says John.

To say it in a similar way for our own time, M. Scott Peck, in his best-selling book *The Road Less Traveled*, says that it is one thing to believe in a nice old God who will take good care of us from his lofty position. But, says psychiatrist Peck, it is quite another to believe in a God who wants us to attain his position, his power, his wisdom, his identity. Peck then adds that most of us do not want to work that hard (p. 280ff). We don't want the responsibility for changing and growing.

Judgment, divine judgment, is essential for our spiritual growth. If the master musician critiques his student, it is for her good. If the master artist critiques his student, it is for his good. If the master teacher critiques his students, it is for their good. If parents critique their children, it can be for their good. And if God critiques us, he means it for our good, for our growth, for our development, for our maturity. Acceptance of God's judgment is one way to prepare for Christmas.

II

Another way to prepare for Christmas is *confession*.

While Roman Catholics continue the confessional and while Orthodox, Catholic, and many Protestant liturgies contain regular prayers of confession, many Protestants have shunned the notion of confession. If our theological forefather John Calvin, following Saint Augustine, suggested all human beings were totally depraved and capable of no human good, later theologians tended to follow the Enlightenment idea of the potential goodness of all human beings.

And while Neo-orthodoxy, overwhelmed with the evils and atrocities of this century, reintroduced the tragic dimension of sin, the various pop-psychology and self-help movements have reasserted the potential goodness of all humans which should be realized and actualized.

Consequently, it is popular in our time not to confess any sin whatsoever. If in his popular novel *Love Story* Erich Segal could define love as never having to say, "I'm sorry," Ogden Nash could whimsically write matrimonial advice which advocated confession for husbands but not for wives:

> *To keep your marriage brimming*
> *With love in the loving cup,*
> *Whenever you're wrong, admit it;*
> *Whenever you're right, shut up.*
> — *I Wouldn't Have Missed It*, p. 334

In a more serious vein, Dr. Scott Peck observes that much of our psychological and spiritual illness is related to our defense mechanisms and denials of any faults or wrongdoing. When we do that we limit our self-awareness, says Peck. "If in our laziness and fear of suffering we massively defend our awareness, then it will come to pass that our understanding of the world will bear little or no relation to reality," says Peck (*op. cit.*, p. 290).

If Dr. Peck advocates self-awareness and confession, so does another prominent psychiatrist, Dr. Karl Menninger. In his well-known and oft-quoted book, *Whatever Became of Sin?* Dr. Menninger notes that most everyone agrees that the world is in terrible shape, but at the same time no one admits to doing anything wrong. And, of course, one reason many of us fear admitting to any wrong is our fear we will be scapegoated for all the wrongs of the world or the workplace or the family. Many people are willing to confess, "He did it," or "She's responsible."

Nevertheless, John the Baptist urges us to prepare for the coming of the Christ by confessing *our* wrongs, *our* sins, to Almighty God. How can we receive the Christ in a wholesome way if we are self-deceptive and self-defensive? If we are quick to condemn our neighbor's wrong and ready always to rationalize our own, how can we receive him who is the embodiment of truth and authenticity?

And then, once confession is made to God, we may have the grace and courage to confess our sins to one another, at least in the family, where we should, as Paul says, be tenderhearted, forgiving one another, as God for Christ's sake forgives us. Confession is good preparation for Christmas.

18

III

Lastly, to prepare for Christmas we should be willing to *repent.*

You will notice that none of these Christmas preparations is as popular as food and presents and parties. You may even find these ideas repugnant, except possibly for other people. Most all of us can think of people who need judgment, who really need to be told off.

And can we not think of people who need to confess their wrongs, especially their wrongs to us? And we can all think of people who need to repent, to change their ways of thinking and acting. Many of us have left church saying to ourselves, I sure hope that sermon hit home with those who needed it.

And yet John the Baptist did not call for repentance for just the other guy or gal. He demanded visible and invisible change from each of his hearers. He was not advocating some simple and sentimental acts of penitence. He did not prescribe some simple good deeds. Instead, he demanded *metanoia*, a complete change of mind and thought patterns and activity.

Or as Scott Peck puts it, when people refuse to repent, "they choose rather to be sick and have the gods to blame than to be well with no one ever to blame again" (*ibid.*, p. 296). He says that those who have faced their problems, accepting responsibility for making the necessary changes, "find themselves not only cured and free from the curses of their childhood and ancestry but also find themselves living in a new and different world" (*ibid.*). These are they who have used their problems as opportunities to repent, to change, to begin a new way of life. These are they who have learned to use even depression and anxiety attacks as a means for change.

Repentance is a way of accepting God's grace for a new way of life. After all, John the Baptist was preaching his message of judgment, confession, and repentance, not because he hated people, but because he cared about people. John was not presenting a God concerned essentially about destroying people, but about saving people. It was not John's intent to thwart our humanity, but to release it for the larger purposes of God's kingdom.

Scott Peck puts it well when he affirms the power of God's love and grace to enable us to accept judgment, to confess our wrongs, and to change our ways. Says Peck, "It is because of grace that it is possible for people to transcend the traumas of loveless parenting and become themselves loving individuals who have risen far above their parents ..." (*ibid.*, p. 300). Or as one young wife and mother put it, "I decided to stop being angry with my dad, blaming him for all my wrongs, and to forgive him and accept him. And now we have a beautiful relationship."

There could hardly be any better preparation for Christmas than that — a time of reconciliation and love in families. But John would remind us amid all the tinsel and toys that the best way to prepare for Christ's coming is to accept his judgment, confess our sins, and repent — make a real change for the better.

Prayer

Eternal Lord God, in this season when the mysteries of life blow about us again like a gentle night breeze on the beach; in this time when our minds are aroused again to wonder and awe, and our hearts softened by the tenderness of the newborn babe; we draw aside to this place holy with memory and aspiration to praise you.

We confess how easily we are caught up in obsession with moneymaking. We acknowledge how readily we ignore our finer human impulses to keep our too-hectic schedules. Time keeps flying by and we too late realize how much of life we are missing, how many opportunities for loving have eluded us, how we have put off those special family times, how easily we have ignored our children or parents, how readily we sacrifice the important, lasting human things for the ephemeral, the fleeting. By your mercy and grace, Lord God, forgive us these missed opportunities. And by your gracious Spirit embolden us to begin anew the adventures of faith and hope and love.

In the Advent season, we beseech you, Lord of the universe, come to us again, as you have come to your people of the past. How often we have wondered about life and death. How perplexed we have become with disease and evil. Violence and brutality abound, injustices, deceit, and hypocrisy seem so prevalent. The tragedies of life, the suffering, the reverses sometimes overwhelm us, and we wonder about life's meaning, looking for answers.

We pray then for your coming, Lord — your coming to those who are suffering and bowed down with the burdens of life, to those bruised, broken, and defeated. We pray for your coming to the seekers of wisdom and truth, and your presence to all hearts in need of love. Through Jesus Christ our Lord. Amen.

A God Who Comes To Us

John 1:6-8, 19-28

It all happened in the Gulf of Mexico. Glenda and her husband Bob had gone out into the Gulf some distance to spear fish. Glenda dived in and shortly began to feel herself carried away by the powerful currents. Responding to her call for help, Bob dived in and swam to her rescue, only to be followed by their little poodle, Spunky. At his wife's insistence Bob swam off to rescue Spunky, and then with great difficulty brought the poodle back to his wife.

However, by now, the swift currents had carried them even further from their boat, which was looking smaller and smaller over the increasingly heavy sea. Although an expert swimmer, Bob knew he could not pull his wife to the boat against the current. And since she had a snorkel and swim fins, he felt she was in no immediate danger. So he started out for the boat, which by now was barely visible. It was not until six long hours later, nearly exhausted, that he was able to reach his boat.

He radioed for help and soon a shrimp fleet, the Coast Guard, and private craft joined in the search for Glenda, who now was lost. Darkness came on and the search became nearly futile. But Glenda continued to remain afloat. She had remembered her husband's advice: remain calm, don't fight the water, raise your head only to breathe. He also had warned her that she might not be able to hold the poodle very long. Eventually, little Spunky became uncontrollably frightened, threatening Glenda's life, so she had to let him go.

Glenda wondered how long she could endure. She was not sure if Bob had made it back to the boat. Shark attacks were a real possibility, and in the darkness a squall had built up. Dehydration caused a powerful thirst; deep sores were developing on her feet around the swim fins; her body temperature began to drop. After the storm, she dozed, using the sea for a pillow, drawing air from her snorkel, which remained above the water. Later little needle-teeth fish nipped at her, causing worry once again that her blood might attract sharks. As the sun began to rise, she judged she had been in the water for at least eighteen hours. She wondered if she should end it all, if help ever would come.

On shore, twenty miles away, searchers collected, including ruddy-faced Duncan MacRae, who had spent fifty years sailing and studying the Gulf. He knew the tides and current and winds. Watch for a flash, he told his men as they neared the area where he calculated Glenda to be. After dashing after several glimmering bottles and cans and other debris, they finally spotted her. She was alive!

They lifted her into the boat. "Thank God," she breathed. "Thank God." She began to weep, as did the three men in the boat. Thank God, help had come. After twenty hours in the water, help had come. After she had lost twenty pounds from dehydration, help had come. After she had prayed and endured, help had come.

In a profound way humankind approaching the twenty-first century finds itself in nihilistic, desperate, life-threatening situations like Glenda, and it asks, "Will help come?" The ancient Jewish exiles of Isaiah's time in 550 B.C. asked themselves over and over again in their Babylonian captivity, "Will help come?" Often they lamented:

> *By the waters of Babylon,*
> *There we sat down and wept,*
> *When we remembered Zion.*
> — Psalm 137:1

Believing themselves to be God's people, now they found themselves in captivity wondering: "Will help come? Will God come

24

to us? Will he send a deliverer to free us up, save us from death, and bring us home?"

Yes, says the prophet Isaiah. We have a God who comes to us, who aids us and helps us in our desperation. And six centuries later on the banks of the Jordan River, John the Baptist, quoting Isaiah, made the same assertion. We have a God who comes to us, and I am the "voice in the wilderness" to prepare the way of the Lord's coming, said John. And standing in the great prophetic tradition John the Baptist says with Isaiah that God comes to us in at least three ways.

I

In the first place, we have a God who comes to us in creation, says Isaiah.

Do you not know, have you not heard,
were you not told long ago,
have you not perceived ever since the world began,
that God sits throned ...
　　He stretches out the skies like a curtain ...
Lift up your eyes to the heavens;
consider who created it all,
led out their host one by one
and called them all by their names;
　　through his great might, his might and power,
　　not one is missing.

— Isaiah 40:21, 22, 26

The majesty, complexity, order, and infinity of the universe are his, says Isaiah. He, by the word of his power, brings it into being and sustains it. Do you think, therefore, that you are too much for him to remember, Isaiah asks his fellow exiles in Babylonia.

Perhaps we, like the ancient Jews, need to be advised to look up into the heavens more often. Harlow Shapley, the late Harvard astronomer, advises us to do that. Note, for example the Big Dipper, the common constellation visible to us all. "The Dipper's bowl," says Shapley, looks very empty, "but the large photographic telescopes reveal many millions of stars in the area which it bounds.

25

More striking," Shapley continues, "is the fact that through the bowl (of the Dipper) the Harvard telescopes have found more than 1,500 distant galaxies" (*Beyond The Observatory*, p. 133).

He then asks us to note two additional facts: "The giant Hale 200-inch telescope on Mount Palomar could easily record the images of a million galaxies in the bowl of the Big Dipper; and since the average stellar population is something like ten billion stars per galaxy, there are many more than ten million billion stars in that small area of the sky" (*ibid.*, pp.133-134).

> *O Lord, our Lord,*
> *how majestic is Thy name in all the earth!*
> *When I look at Thy heavens,*
>   *the work of Thy fingers,*
> *The moon and the stars which*
>   *Thou hast established;*
> *What is man that Thou art mindful of him,*
> *and the son of man that Thou dost care for him?*
>   — Psalm 8:1, 3-4

Of course many people would claim he doesn't. God is indifferent they say; he pays no attention. The world goes on its way by its own laws, and God ignores it. Jewish exiles six centuries before Christ were thinking that. Many people since have been thinking that. But Isaiah and John and the whole Biblical tradition assert the opposite. By the faithfulness of the created world, by its order and pattern, seasons and cycles, seed-time and harvest, by the miracle of conception and birth, God is coming to us, sustaining and helping us.

When we get discouraged, Isaiah and John would tell us to look up and out at the majesty of the universe. Or look inward through the microscope and watch the vital secrets of life do their faithful work, all by the hand of God. We have a God who comes to us in creation.

II

In the second place, Isaiah saw the coming of God in the international political events of his time.

The Babylonian Empire which had conquered the little country of Judah and carried her inhabitants into exile was beginning to have its problems. After the death of Babylon's King Nebuchadnezzar, a good deal of political intrigue occurred. Eventually, Cyrus the Persian defeated the Medes and Lydians and pressed on to overwhelm Babylonia.

Isaiah saw, in the rise of Cyrus to power, the hand of God. Fully aware of the international situation, Isaiah saw in the political and military events the movement of God's Spirit. The purposes and achievements of God were developing with world leaders. In fact, Isaiah was so enthusiastic that he called Cyrus God's shepherd and even went so far as to announce him as God's Messiah, his Christ. Cyrus did in fact become that for the exiled Jews, for he did release them to return to their homeland. Furthermore, he encouraged them to set up their own government, to reestablish their economy, to rebuild their temple, and to revitalize their religion. No wonder then that Cyrus has been called one of history's most enlightened rulers. No wonder Isaiah would refer to him as a kind of Christ. God had come to them in a world leader not of their nation or religion. And Isaiah had announced his Advent.

Standing in the tradition of Isaiah, we too look for the repeated coming of God in historical events. We believe God loves the world, cares about its people, and longs for a just and righteous life on the face of the earth. Like Isaiah, we believe "God moves in mysterious ways his wonders to perform," that sometimes in the strangest places and people, he works his will.

What are the signs of God's advent in contemporary history? Could it be that the immense pendulum swing to mysticism and classical romanticism is a sign of the search for God, the longing for his coming into a materialistic, technologically preoccupied society? Could it be that the drug culture is in part a search for another kind of experience, a peace and transcendence not unlike the religious experience? And let me remind you that some of the biggest drug users are not American sons and daughters, but American fathers and mothers with barbiturates and assorted tranquilizers. Have a problem? Then pop a pill. It's the "valley of the dolls."

Does God come to us in history? Could it be that the charismatic movement, the Holy Spirit movement, is God's way of coming to a materialistically stuffed but spiritually starved culture? Is it God's way of moving in history, claiming a new people for his own, enriching them with a spiritual joy and peace that tranquilizers, barbiturates, and alcohol cannot begin to touch? Is it God's way of saying to a despairing world, "I have not forsaken you, I will raise up new Cyruses, I will renew the power of my living Christ in the world, I will not leave you alone?"

Is not God working among us in the peace negotiations? In the new and enlightened treaties? In the disarmament talks? In new and better trade agreements? In this Advent season could not God be saying to us in the poetry of Isaiah:

> You who bring Zion good news, up with you to the
>   mountaintop;
> lift up your voice and shout,
> you who bring good news to Jerusalem,
>   lift it up fearlessly;
> cry to the cities of Judah, "Your God is here."
> Here is the Lord God coming in might,
>   coming to rule with his right arm.
>   His recompense comes with him,
>   He carries his reward before him.
> He will tend his flock like a shepherd
>   and gather them together with his arm;
> He will carry the lambs in his bosom
>   and lead the (young lambs) to water.
>   — Isaiah 40:9-11

It is a time to shout, to celebrate, to announce the good tidings of great joy that we have a God who comes to us in the movements and events of history, who takes our individual puniness and sweeps it along in the overwhelming streams of his love and spirit. By signs and wonders outside ourselves, outside our power and control, he comes to us, making his purposes known, defeating the threatening nihilism and despair.

Look then this Advent for a God who works to break apart the rigid encrustations of stuffy religion. Look for a God who challenges flaccid commitment and anemic devotion. Look for a God who executes judgment on institutions that are more concerned with their own preservation than with the people they are supposed to serve. Look for a God who challenges established but unjust authorities and corrupt vested interests. Look for a God whose Spirit is brooding over the depths of human wretchedness, whose seeing eye points out the rape and waste of the earth, whose penetrating word cuts into corporations and professions, exposing deceit, uncovering deception, executing judgment.

We have a God who comes to us in the circumstances of history, whose Spirit and Mind manifest themselves in historical movements and events, whose heart pulsates in every movement for human justice, in every cause of social righteousness. He who has eyes to see what is happening in our time, let him see. He who has ears to hear, let him hear. We have a God who comes to us.

III

In the third place, we have a God who comes to us in a person far greater than Isaiah's Cyrus. We have a God who manifests himself to us in a great deliverer and leader, one who is more esteemed than Alexander the Great or Caesar Augustus, far more righteous than Judas Maccabaeus or Constantine, infinitely more brotherly than a Napoleon and charismatic than a Patton, wiser than a MacArthur and more just than an Eisenhower. I speak, of course, of Jesus.

Even the great John the Baptist confessed he was not the Christ, but the "voice in the wilderness" preparing the way for the coming of Christ. Said John, "I baptize with water; but among you stands one whom you do not know, even he who comes after me, the thong of whose sandal I am not worthy to untie" (John 1:26-27). He too was, of course, speaking of Jesus.

And in Jesus, we see God coming to us, ironically. Expecting to see pomp in God's chosen one, we see humility. Anticipating majesty, we discover a servant. Looking for royalty, we find someone close to peasantry. Hoping for grandeur, we experience grace.

29

Desiring the power for vengeance, we are given the power of forgiveness. Longing for a world ruler who would lead us to world domination, we find a world leader who leads us to world service. Expecting his leadership in a war to end all wars, we hear his call to beat our swords into plowshares and our spears into pruning hooks. Craving a conqueror to crush the opposition, we find a counselor for peace and the love of enemies. Wishing a victor to vanquish the foe, we discover a victim who suffers in behalf of the foe. Anticipating violence, we find powerful love. Expecting brutal force on God's behalf, we experience instead the force of forgiveness, acceptance, and inclusion.

We have a God who comes to us in Jesus. We have a God whose mind, whose logos or reason, was received into, and exhibited by, Jesus of Nazareth. In Jesus, all our theories and abstractions about God, all our easy philosophies and afternoon wonderings, all our vain tale-spinning and wish-dreaming — all these fanciful notions about God are grounded and given concrete reality. With Jesus, God is not some ethereal dream or esoteric vapor, but the eternal Father to whom he gives his unflagging allegiance. Jesus, when he speaks of God, puts his money where his mouth is. He comes out of the comfortable clouds of idle speculation to put his body where his convictions are. Jesus leaves the vain world of obsessive introspection to put his very life on the line in obedience to God and service to men. So much so, that the very life and light of God shine through him so that he illuminates and revitalizes all those who come near him. In this Advent we celebrate and announce that we have a God who comes to us through Jesus.

The question then is this: Is God coming to you?

Doctors know that there are many people who still refuse to come to them. They refuse to acknowledge their sickness and their need for a doctor. It is difficult for them to confess their dependency, their lack of self-sufficiency. Believing themselves to be adequate for everything, they never have learned to receive help graciously. Finally, however, they send for the rescue squad, which comes clanging in desperation.

Advent is more than a rescue squad operation. It proposes regular visits and check-ups with God, the Divine Physician, who

30

wants to keep us in continuing good health. It suggests opening up the self to nature, to history, to Jesus. Advent proposes repentance, a change of loyalties and habits, a new openness to the presence of God in our midst. Do not make the tragic error of mistaking God's servanthood for servility or his humility for weakness. He does not come as a genie to the beck and call of our slightest selfish whim.

But to those who confess their sin and acknowledge their need of God to straighten out and revitalize their decrepit lives, God still comes. He comes to us if we open ourselves to him to receive his professional care, and, like Glenda, will rescue us from despair.

As Phillips Brooks, the famous preacher of the last century, put it:

> *How silently, how silently,*
> *The wondrous gift is given!*
> *So God imparts to human hearts*
> *The blessings of his heaven.*
> *No ear may hear his coming,*
> *But in this world of sin,*
> *Where meek souls will receive him,*
> *Still the dear Christ enters in.*

Prayer

Eternal God, in the beauty of this place and the inspiration of this hour, we draw aside unto you as sheep who would come into the more immediate presence of their shepherd. Even as we do so, we find that we must readily acknowledge ourselves as sheep who have gone astray, who, wandering about in the wide range of the world's activity, have lost their way. So we come to you, O Father, we come to you sometimes lonely and despairing, sometimes bruised and scarred, other times hardened and cynical. Yet we come, partly because we cannot stay away. Although many times we may deny it, deep down we sense our need for you. Many times we have thought ourselves to be self-sufficient, only to be caught in moments of embarrassing inadequacy. So we come to you, O God, confessing our dependence, believing we are happiest and most complete when we live in cooperative harmony with you.

We thank you, O Lord God, for the season of Advent and its reminder of your faithful concern for us. We ask you once again in this season to enlarge our vision and renew within us a driving sense of purpose for your Kingdom. Deliver us from all the little things which enslave us and keep us from the larger aims of your Kingdom. Draw us out of the preoccupation with ourselves which is vanity. Save us from the entanglements of picayune peeves and the bondage to pettiness. Lift us from the quicksand of perpetual negative thinking to the exciting possibilities for ourselves and humankind.

We come to you out of many moods and circumstances, O God. Some come out of bitterness and envy. Give them a great sense of forgiveness and compassion, we pray. Some come out of solitariness and self-pity. Grant them the realization that they are not alone in either their joy or their suffering. Some come out of pride of success and a boastful spirit. May they experience the true strength of character which is humility as exhibited in the Christ. Some come out of desperation, grant them hope; some come out of doubt, help them doubt their doubts; some come out of smallness of heart, enlarge their compassion; some come out of mourning and trouble, grant them comfort and courage. All of us come out of great need; grant us help, we pray.

We pray not only for ourselves, but for your people and all the world. Especially do we ask your emotional blessings upon all negotiations for peace. Work your will in the minds and spirits of all world leaders, that peace might prevail.

Give our land, in this season, a new birth of courage, a new gift of integrity, a new sense of resolve for justice; that peace and good will toward all men might prevail throughout the earth. Through Jesus Christ our Lord. Amen.

Kingdom Without End

Luke 1:26-38

"I'm the luckiest son-of-gun that ever was born," said the late Senator Barry Goldwater of Arizona, who served five terms in the Senate before retiring in 1986. Goldwater, grandson of a Jewish immigrant peddler, successful businessman, and one-time Republican presidential candidate, thought our country is in trouble.

It is in trouble, he once said in an interview, because of the sad state of the Senate and Congress. Goldwater lamented the passing of giants in the Senate like Walter George, Richard Russell, Bob Taft, and Loehman of New York. Never one to mince words, he added, "Today we have a bunch of bums running for office. We have a Congress that should not be allowed *any* place."

More than that, when he was a boy, "A man's word was all you needed," said Goldwater. Our forefathers were immigrants who were honest and wanted to work, he said. Even today we have young people coming out west who are much like the immigrants. Then again, with his usual opinionated candor, Goldwater said, "We don't have a lot of bums and crooks and typical Easterners moving out here. To me, the difference about those days was decency and honesty."

But Goldwater doesn't lay all this country's problems on the shoulders of "bums from the East." He said, "Every country that has failed in the history of the world has failed because of the same things we are doing in America today." He added that if we don't make a decided change in the deficit, the country will be bankrupt in ten years.

He admitted it was a terrible thing to say about a country which has enjoyed so much prosperity and so many privileges. Nevertheless, he was hopeful about the young people he taught at universities. He saw them as different from their fathers and mothers. He then added: "I hope I'm wrong, but the way this country's going today, we haven't got that long" (*Parade*, Nov. 28, 1993, pp. 4-6).

If Goldwater sounded pessimistic from the conservative side of the aisle, similar feelings can be expressed from the more liberal side. For example, Henry Cisneros, at one time the Secretary for Housing and Urban Development, lamented how gridlocked the bureaucratic system is in Washington. It's difficult to get anything done through the massive governmental machinery to address such pressing needs as homelessness in this country. We have a permanent underclass. Violence and drive-by shootings are becoming commonplace, said Cisneros. Then Cisneros added: "I came to this job because I believe that time is running out on the American way of life as we know it" (*Time*, Dec. 6, 1993, p. 31).

If from both sides of the political aisle Cisneros and Goldwater seem overly pessimistic, Will and Ariel Durant can speak from the perspective of history. After completing their ten-volume history, *The Story Civilization*, they wrote a little sequel titled *The Lessons of History*. Most all civilizations eventually decline and decay, say the Durants. They begin, flourish, decline, and disappear.

Perhaps Shelley said it best when he wrote his famous poem:

> *I met a traveler from an antique land*
> *Who said: Two vast and trunkless legs of stone*
> *Stand in the desert. Near them, on the sand,*
> *Half sunk, a shattered visage lies, whose frown,*
> *And wrinkled lip, and sneer of cold command,*
> *Tell that its sculptor well those passions read.*
> *Which yet survive, stamped on these lifeless things,*
> *The hand that mocked them and the heart that fed:*
> *And on the pedestal these words appear:*
> *"My name is Ozymandias, king of kings:*
> *Look on my works, ye Mighty, and despair!"*

Nothing beside remains. Round the decay
Of that colossal wreck, boundless and bare.
The lone and level sands stretch far away.

Will that be said of America? Will that be said of your favorite "kingdom," that society or group or organization or corporation in which you find meaning and identity? Will, after all is said and done, our civilization, our family, our business, our corporation, our little kingdom lie boundless and bare with the lone and level sands stretching far away? Yes. Yes, they will. That is why in this season we come to set our faith and hope on a kingdom that will never end.

I

The kingdom of Christ will have no end because *it is focused more on the future than the past.*

To be sure, the angel Gabriel announced to Mary that her son would indeed be given the throne of his father David. He was to reign over Israel forever. At first glance it seemed as though Gabriel was predicting a restoration of the past.

Luke may have been reflecting that popular sentiment in his Gospel. It was true that the reign of David a thousand years earlier was looked upon as the Golden Age of Israel. It was true that many of the popular expectations regarding the Messianic Kingdom envisioned David's successor on the throne in the palace in Jerusalem. It was hoped they could restore the bygone years and return to the glorious past. Many people had a backward look to God.

But not Jesus. "No man putting his hand to the plow and looking back is fit for the Kingdom of God," said Jesus. You must concentrate more on what lies ahead than upon what you have accomplished, says Jesus. If you are the kind of person always waiting around to bury the previous generation before you enter the next one, you are not fit for God's Kingdom, said Jesus.

Thomas Wolfe has told us we cannot go home again. It is impossible to return to the peak experiences of history and expect we will relive them in all their glory and meaning. Nostalgia and

35

sentiment may be nice moods for holidays, but they are not the energy of the kingdom without end. Hope and faith in the God of the future provide that.

Historians Will and Ariel Durant said, "There is no certainty that the future will repeat the past. Every year is an adventure" (*The Lessons of History*, p. 88). They then add significantly, "When the group or a civilization declines, it is through no mystic limitation of a corporate life, but through the failure of its political or intellectual leaders to meet the challenges of change" (*ibid.*, p. 92).

Change was precisely what Jesus represented. It became more and more apparent that he wished for something more than a restoration of the past glory of David's kingdom. Observing the endless and vicious cycle of revenge and counter-revenge, distressed with the violence and brutality characteristic of most world empires, he looked to a future where people would share in the fabulous wealth and beauty of the earth and live peaceably and constructively rather than violently and destructively.

After all, David's kingdom was founded on war and violence. The admiring women of David's time had their song that told it all: "King Saul has killed his thousands, King David has killed his tens of thousands."

Restore that kind of kingdom? Re-create that kind of violence, bloodshed, and terror? That's the way of the brutal, self-annihilating past. "Put away your sword," Jesus told Peter after he had cut off the high priest's servant's ear in the Garden of Gethsemane. "They who live by the sword, die by the sword." If we resort to military power, my kingdom will be over as soon as the next greater military power comes along.

Christ's kingdom will never end because it accepts the challenge of a new future rather than re-creating a violent past.

II

Christ's kingdom will never end because it rests more on *faith than fixity*. It is flexible rather than rigid.

Many people's idea of the perfect kingdom or group is one which looks an awful lot like themselves. Prior to Jesus' time, his own people had developed a high sense of religious and moral exclusivism. Many of his own people had moved from thinking of themselves as God's chosen or *elect* people to thinking of themselves as God's *elite* people. Their definition of the true insider grew smaller and smaller until God's kingdom was smothered in the snobbish conceits of a few people well content in their ancestral and social and religious credentials. In other words, being in this kingdom depended little on what you yourself believed or did. Rather, it was largely a matter of resting on the genes and deeds of your ancestors.

Interestingly, one of the recent arguments for faith over fixity comes from a surprising quarter, from George Gilder's popular book, *Wealth and Poverty*. He says that in order to make progress out of poverty people need to have a good family life, they need to work hard, and they need, above all, to have faith. He says, "Faith in man, faith in the future, faith in the rising returns of giving ... faith in the providence of God are all essential to successful capitalism" (p. 73).

Gilder goes on to add that "a world without innovation succumbs to the sure laws of deterioration and decay" (p. 260). And in order to innovate, we have to believe that something new is possible. We have to be intuitive and imaginative. We have to be able to envision new realities and risk new dreams. We cannot, says Gilder, always "look before we leap." That is possible only when we assume the permanence and fixity of the present order of things.

We cannot fully grasp a new reality from the perspective of the old. We have to take risks and make the "leap of faith." We have to believe, says Gilder, in the cosmic mystery, in the Mind of God. Many people, he says, are "frozen by fear on the thresholds of higher consciousness" (p. 264). We are afraid to take risks, to take chances. We want to define the future by the past. We want to arrest progress so we can control our little paradise, our little niche of the good life.

Some years ago I received regularly the church newsletter of a minister friend of mine. I most always read his pastoral letters, only to discover they were usually about the religious experiences of his childhood or youth. In each issue he seemed to be on a nostalgia trip, bathing in the sentiment of the way things used to be.

When I saw him next I joked with him and chided him about his faith being fixed more in the past than the future. I asked him if he had not had a significant experience in his spiritual formation since childhood.

How about you? Have you had a serious religious experience since your youth or childhood? Have you seriously studied the Bible or theology to discover whether your religious ideas have moved beyond the third grade level? Have you learned a new religious song or hymn in the last five years, or do you insist on singing always your beloved hymns of the distant past? Are you approaching the future more with fear than faith, more with fixity than with flexibility?

Christ's true kingdom will exist forever because it is based on faith over fear, flexibility over fixity. If you are clinging desperately to a receding, distant past, you will be left behind. Take the risk of faith today.

III

Christ's kingdom is without end because it is *primarily spiritual and eternal rather than material and temporal.*

Long ago Jesus told Pilate that if his kingdom were of this world, he would enlist the legions of angels to help him fight. And even before that he told the tempter on the Mount of Temptation that he would not, even for all the kingdoms of the world, give up his true devotion and obedience to God and his everlasting kingdom. Jesus did not say that his kingdom had nothing to do with this world. After all, he taught his disciples to pray, "Thy kingdom come, thy will be done *on earth* as it is in heaven." Yet it was to be a kingdom which transcended time and space.

Once again we turn to George Gilder, who notes astutely that "the only stable asset among the quakes and shadows is a disciplined brain. Matter melts, but mind and will can flash for a while ahead of the uncertain crowd, beam visions across the sky, and induce their incarnation in silicone and cement before the competition gathers." Gilder then adds, "The best, most compelling, most original, and flexible minds constitute the most enduring gold" (*op. cit.,* p. 58).

Nevertheless, even though "matter melts" it is our habit to cling to it firmly, attach ourselves to it with a death grip. For example, we often attach ourselves to our business or corporation. Think how many people find their total identity within the mentality and milieu of one manifestation of business or corporate life. They truly are the corporate man or woman enslaved to that particular configuration of reality. And then when they retire, they are truly lost without identity, becoming soft and puffy, eventually dying prematurely.

Or it may be a nation. Stalin once sneeringly asked how many military divisions the Pope had, but Stalin is dead as is his empire, while Christ's Church lives. The Roman Empire is long gone, as are the Ottoman and the Hapsburg Empires, and the Third Reich too, buried with Ozymandias' dust heap of history — once proud, invincible nations in the dust — as alas, ours may someday be, sooner than we think perhaps. The only kingdom that lasts forever is Christ's kingdom of mind and spirit, never complete in this world, always looking for true fulfillment in the next.

One summer, my wife and I had the privilege of leading a number of our church people on a religious heritage tour of Great Britain. Since our Congregational roots as well as our national roots are to be found there, it was an important and meaningful trip.

Of course, we early on stopped at Westminster Abbey, replete with its glorious architecture and fabulous history. The Abbey, we learned, is directly under the control of the Queen of England, and not the Archbishop of Canterbury.

On the last day of our tour we returned to London, and many of us had resolved to attend Vespers at 5:00 p.m. in the Abbey. Most of us made it in time and actually sat in the choir loft, listening to the sacred words and the heavenly voices of the Men and Boys Choir of the Abbey. It was glorious, sitting there in the presence of hundreds of years of epochal history of the now-depleted British Empire.

It was then I saw it. It was engraved in the chancel, in front of the Abbey where Britain's monarchs had been crowned for years. There they were, these words from the Bible's last book — Revelation. They said, "The Kingdoms of this world have become the kingdom of our Lord and of his Christ." And then that verse goes on to say, "And he shall reign forever and ever."

What king and kingdom do you serve this Christmas season? Have you given your heart and mind to the King of kings, the Lord of lords? Is this not the time to open up to receive him anew as your Lord and Master, and King of kings? This is the season to renew our love and loyalty to the kingdom without end.

Prayer

Almighty God, glorious in majesty, whose domain encompasses the myriad million blazing suns and whose power sustains the whirling galaxies thousands of light-years from our view, we adore and worship you. Your reality is beyond our comprehension, but you grant us a glimpse of your Being from the vistas of insight and revelation. Your mystery is unfathomable, yet you allow us to participate in your very nature, like being in the ocean but never possessing it. We bow before your awesome presence and praise you for all the splendid panoply of the universe.

In the presence of your greatness, it is for us to confess our too frequent smallness. Conscious of your grand scheme of things entire, we acknowledge our obsession with pettiness and trivial pursuits. Forgive our spiritual and intellectual nearsightedness, and lift up our eyes to the more distant horizons and the broader perspective you would have us behold.

In this season when we are reminded of the Christ Child and his spiritual kingdom without end, which even now encompasses the earth and two thousand years, renew our devotion to him and his cause of peace and love and service. Release us from the petty fiefdoms which gain our allegiance. Save us from the tyranny of negative thinking and from slavery to uncontrolled passions. Liberate us from all unworthy masters of our souls and draw us again into your service, which is perfect freedom.

In this season we especially pray for our families and friends, those near and dear ones who enrich our lives and help us to know the meaning of love. Repair by your grace any family hostilities and unresolved angers. Help forgiveness to prevail over grudge

bearing and let the spirit of amendment take precedence over revenge. Bind up the wounds of grief with your balm of Gilead and
infuse all despairing souls with the Spirit of the Christ who came
to conquer death in all its forms, and to bring us into his kingdom
without end. In the name of Christ we pray. Amen.

The Hidden Power Of Small Beginnings

Luke 2:1-14 (15-20)

Jesus was born during the golden age of the Roman Empire, under the reign of Caesar Augustus. The Empire embraced most of Europe, stretched south to Egypt and on into the Far East. The Jewish province of Judea was, of course, included, and Judea's little village of Bethlehem was a grain of sand in the vast sands of humanity subject to Augustus' mighty power.

Powerful as the Roman Empire was at the time of Christ's birth, it was not without serious problems. The institutions of marriage and family were disintegrating, as were the old religious beliefs. Will Durant observes that "the decay of the ancient faith among the upper classes had washed away the supernatural supports of marriage, fidelity, and parentage; the passage from farm to city had made children less of an asset, more of a liability and a toy; women wished to be sexually rather than maternally beautiful; in general the desire for individual freedom seemed to be running counter to the needs of the race" (*Caesar and Christ*, p. 22).

Longing for a stable and vital empire, Augustus attempted religious, moral, and governmental reforms and was moderately successful. Honesty and lawfulness in government bureaucracies were increased. Religious leaders and festivals were encouraged and lavishly supported. Art, architecture, literature, and culture flourished, yet it was not a genuinely creative age, but, says historian H. G. Wells, an age of spending and trade "in which the rich grew richer and the poor poorer and the soul and spirit of man decayed" (*The Outline of History*, p. 458).

Wells goes on to claim that military oppression and self-indulged opulence had stifled honest intellectual inquiry. The Empire "respected wealth and ... despised science. It gave government to the rich, and imagined that wise men could be bought and bargained for in the slave markets when they were needed." Despite the somewhat puritanical reforms of Augustus, "It was," says Wells, "a colossally ignorant and unimaginative empire. They foresaw nothing" (*ibid.*, p. 467).

Who then could have been concerned with the birth of a son to a poor carpenter and his wife? What did the rustic, obscure stable of Bethlehem have to do with the splendid grandeur and enormous power of the Imperial City? After all, it was by the order of Augustus Caesar that Mary and Joseph were going to Bethlehem in the first place. They were complying with the imperial decree demanding a public census. And yet, there was the hidden power of small beginnings wrapped in swaddling cloths, lying in a manger. And within three centuries, the humble King had conquered Rome not by power, not by might, but by the Lord's Spirit.

I

Note first of all the hidden power in small beginnings in our everyday life.

How often have the wise men of the world laughed and scoffed at the new ideas of men who appear to be simpletons? We have learned not to laugh quite so loudly in the scientific realm. New discoveries and new breakthroughs in scientific knowledge tend to keep us humble and open to new truth.

But in the ethical and moral dimensions we tend to be less open and more adamant. Brutal and ruthless exhibits of power usually have won the day in the history of the world, we say. And in many instances we would be right. Yet we persistently overlook the tremendous influence which acts of kindness and humility have had upon our personal lives as well as upon history.

For example, most of us, at some time or other, have been influenced by a playground bully. He pushed his way around, used his brute power to impress us and to get his way. Yet we were influenced more by the acts of kindness and thoughtfulness and camaraderie demonstrated by our friends. Men have known women who were brash and forward, rude and crude. They have power, but what a powerful effect a kind and tender and thoughtful woman can have upon a man. Women have known many men who were big and powerful and handsome, about ninety percent brawn, five percent brain, and five percent heart. Such men make an impression, but add sensitivity, kindness, gentleness, and thoughtfulness to a man, and those so-called "weak" gifts make a powerful impact.

Many of you will remember the story of the huge electrical generator which would not work. Local power plant technicians struggled with the problem but could not get it to run. Finally, they called in an outside expert who carefully examined the generator, and after some deliberation he picked up a hammer and gave the generator a whack, and it started right up.

A few days later the power company received a bill for 2,001 dollars for services rendered. The labor charge was one dollar and professional services were 2,000 dollars. When the power company called the expert to ask for an explanation for the high charges, he put it this way. "The one dollar labor charge is for swinging the hammer. The 2,000 dollars is for knowing where to hit." Such is the hidden power of small, humble things. Often it is the power of quiet insight into the truth, the ability to penetrate to the key idea or concept that makes all the difference in the world.

Likewise there is the hidden power of small things like drops of water. If you want to split a huge rock, do as some of the ancients did. Put a piece of wood into a crack or hole in the rock, pour water on it steadily, and the wood will swell and crack the huge rock. Think also of the power of small drops of water, which freeze and expand and drive apart wood, rocks, and cement with tremendous force. Note the power of the tiny seed or the immense energy of the tiny atom. In the natural world there is hidden power in the small things, from the basic plankton of the food chain of the sea which makes its way eventually into the whales, giving them sustenance, to microscopic seeds and eggs which carry the secrets and power of life from century to century. What fantastic powers in the smallest of things!

II

Note in the second place that God himself, in all his majesty, deals in small and humble things.

In Luke's story, God's revelation of Christ's birth came not to the wise and sophisticated but to humble and unlearned shepherds. The humble often are more ready to receive the essential truths of life than those preoccupied with sophisticated trivia. Like the prophets of old, Jesus often commended the humble, saying, "Blessed are the poor in spirit, for theirs is the Kingdom of God." "Blessed are the meek, for they shall inherit the earth."

Later, Paul emphasized a similar theme. "My brothers, think what sort of people you are, whom God has called. Few of you are men of wisdom, by any human standard; few are powerful or highly born. Yet, to shame the wise, God has chosen what the world counts folly, and to shame what is strong, God has chosen what the world counts weakness. He has chosen things low and contemptible, mere nothings, to overthrow the existing order. And so there is no place for human pride in the presence of God" (1 Corinthians 1:26-30).

This is the precise theme of the Gospels and Paul with respect to Jesus and his birth. In his letter to the Philippians, Paul writes of Christ: "For the divine nature was his from the first; yet he did not think to snatch at equality with God, but made himself nothing, assuming the nature of a slave. Bearing the human likeness, revealed in human shape, he humbled himself, and in obedience accepted even death — death on a cross" (2:6-8).

Therefore, Luke states with great beauty and simplicity one of the central truths of the Christian gospel — namely, that God is able to work through the humble and open and simple people as well as through the worldly wise.

Let me ask you, if you were planning the details of a royal birth of a man who would change the history of the entire world, how would you do it? Cleanest hospital and best doctors, right? Surely not a stable among the animals! And would you not arrange for the birth to be of a very proper Eastern family, with impeccable pedigree and Social Register listing from the beginning?

And we would need wealth, prestige, and manly good looks, combining Marlon Brando, Clark Gable, and Christopher Reeve into some kind of super-male. And the right schools would be important — boarding schools and colleges and the very best of graduate schools. Further, we would be careful that such an important personage be protected from every hazard, every danger, every threat to physical and psychological well-being. Careful diet, regular medical attention, beautiful clothes, comely friends, and correct social circles would be mandatory for our royalty who is to change the world.

Such are the ways of men, but not very often the ways of God. God takes greater risks than man. His unique Son is born in a stable with no doctors in attendance, perhaps not even a midwife. Jesus grew up without the attention and flattery of a royal court. He went to synagogue school with the other boys of his hometown, Nazareth. In Jerusalem there were many pretenders to the throne, young men properly educated with the right teachers and important acquaintances. They knew the intricacies of political and religious infighting. Comparatively speaking, they were of proper pedigree and social standing, with authenticated genealogy. But Nazareth, despicable Nazareth of the Gentile north, can anything good come out of Nazareth? Such was the question most on the lips of polite Jerusalem circles and entrenched political and religious powers of the capital city.

When Jesus was asked for his credentials he had none, except the credentials he gave to the followers of John the Baptist. "Go and tell John," he said, "what you hear and see: the blind recover their sight, the lame walk, the lepers are made clean, the deaf hear, the dead are raised to life, the poor are hearing the good news — and happy is the man who does not find me a stumbling block" (Matthew 11:4-6).

But many did find him a stumbling block. "Where are your credentials?" they asked repeatedly. But they were looking for man's credentials — degrees, genealogies, connections, letters of recommendation, proper background, worldly sophistication, ability to command armies and men. But Jesus kept repeating the credentials of God, credentials not of static status, but of dynamic action.

People who were blind see. Those who were deaf hear. The lame walk and the poor and humble are not neglected, but are given equal time.

Oh God, how wise you are. How disarming to men. How simple and yet how powerful are your hidden ways. Men try to make their kingdoms by force; even the Kingdom of God has been subjected to violence and violent men, and yet you come to us so humbly, so innocently, making yourself and your plans so vulnerable, so open to threat and annihilation, and yet so pervasively powerful. What splendor! What wisdom! What majesty! What love! The King of the Universe comes to his servants as a servant. Oh, the hidden power of small beginnings.

III

In the third place, even in the worst of times, small beginnings have hidden power.

One reason why small beginnings have such hidden power is due to the very fact of their smallness. They are unpretentious. They do not threaten us. A tiny baby melts the cynicism and hardness of heart of the most recalcitrant men. A man may have slain his thousands in battle and surpassed his hundreds in business or profession, but let a little baby reach out to him with tender hand and gentle smile, and he has been won over.

Another reason small beginnings have power is their apparent innocence. Few of us can assign sinister motives to babies or to new, struggling ideas and institutions. Consequently, in the presence of smallness and its apparent innocence, we drop our defenses, are more open and receptive, and thus are more likely to come under the influence of the small and little.

Still another reason small ideas have such hidden power is that their potential is not plainly seen. If people surrounding the birth of Alexander the Great or Augustus Caesar or Dwight Eisenhower had realized the tremendous potential in each of those babies, they might have taken more notice. As it was, the hidden power of their potential developed gradually, to the point where, of course, everyone took notice!

Small beginnings, unpretentious, non-threatening beginnings, have great power to influence our lives, because we tend to be open and receptive to them. Besides, many of us do not seem to have the capacity to comprehend the huge and complex factors of life. For example, think for a moment of the budget meeting of any church or corporation or organization. Very often we become "penny wise and pound foolish"! We will quibble over a ten-dollar item here or a 25-dollar item there and let go unnoticed the several thousand-dollar item. Why? Because everyone understands pennies and dollars and knows how to save them. But when it comes to thousands of dollars, many people are lost. The small has influence because it's understood. The large often passes by uncomprehended.

Likewise, in the religious dimension. We may go through a large religious service and have all the hymns and scriptures and sermons go unnoticed until one parishioner smiles and speaks to another, or until a little act of kindness is done, or until someone is helped in a little way. While the large official and formal acts of religion have their important place, it often is the little things of religion that mean a lot. They help in little ways where help is needed. And very often the real power behind churches is the hidden power of a million small beginnings — small beginnings of praying for one another, sharing with one another, giving generously to the financial needs of the Church, teaching and leading in education and youth programs — these and innumerable other small beginnings eventually, like the seeds of winter, blossom into a springtime of powerful beauty and wonder.

Even in the worst of times these small beginnings are going on. Not long ago, I learned a surprising fact — a fact known to foresters and naturalists for years, but unknown to me. I learned that in many places forest fires are essential for the continuing life of the forest. In fact, if lightning did not regularly start the fires, man would have to do so. Why? Because the new seed settled into the forest floor needs the intense heat of the fire to cause it to germinate. Without the fire, the seeds would remain dormant and eventually the forest would die.

Actually, it is very similar in the society of men. There are many dormant seeds of potential hidden in the hearts and minds of men, and very often only the intense heat of social crisis will cause them to germinate. Remember the black lady, Rosa Parks, who refused in Montgomery, Alabama, to go to the back of the bus? That small beginning produced a social heat that gave great impetus to Martin Luther King, Jr., and others. It was just a few short years ago that Governor George Wallace stood in the doorway of the University of Alabama, blocking the entrance of black students. But not long ago, he crowned a black homecoming queen at that same school. What hidden power in small beginnings in the heart and mind of a black woman in a Montgomery, Alabama, bus. And out of the resulting fire of social crisis, a million new seeds of hope sprung into life for repressed American blacks.

Therefore, we should always live in hope. At this moment, God is preparing new men with new ideas to give badly needed, religiously enlightened, moral leadership to our land. If we are honest, if we stand up like men and confess our wrongs, if we come clean with God, and insist on justice, righteousness, and integrity, he will not forsake us. But if we shuffle our feet, cringe in dark corners like cowards, constantly rationalizing our sin and immorality, we can expect no mercy from God. And the new life he always promises to the world will pass us by.

God always has a remnant of people ready to do his will. In every century and country he always has a few who have not bowed the knee to Baal, who have not idolized sex, money, and pleasure, who have not made perpetual excuses for their immorality and injustice. Even now, people — men and women — are being prepared to give us leadership — small beginnings of hidden power out of the ashes of a burned-over and purified social order; new seedlings of life are breaking through.

It is a time of hope. It is a time of hidden power in small beginnings.

Prayer
Almighty God, who with quietness and holiness comes into the lives of people ready to receive you, and who satisfies with plenty the longing heart and thirsting soul, we come to you for

encouragement and sustenance. How glad we are for your patient ways with humankind. Year after year, century after century, you bear patiently with us until we grow and mature and develop, gradually learning the things which make for peace and fulfillment. Our history is so full of strife and war, scandal and bloodshed, but in this season we come seeking new visions for peace and goodwill, and new strength to make our visions realities.

O God, in this season we pray for peace in our many relationships. May grudges long harbored in our hearts be melted by new rays of love. Let bitterness and envy vanish, and hope and joy take their place. May all wandering sons and daughters find their way back to the home circle and the Father's forgiveness. Let the lonely and forgotten ones find a friend, and help those burdened with many anxieties find release and reassurance. For those weary in well-doing we ask a new measure of encouragement by seeing the fruits of their many labors.

As always, O loving Father, we ask that the Spirit of Christ be reborn in our hearts. We believe something new came into the world with him. Let us do away then with old and useless rivalries. Help us to be done with vain ambitions and perverted longings. Redirect our thoughts and affections that they may be more in keeping with your Peaceable Kingdom. Save us from despair, and keep us from cynicism. Through Jesus Christ our Lord. Amen.

The Child That Changed The World

Luke 2:22-40

Eight days after his birth Jesus was circumcised according to Jewish law and custom. It was then he was officially given the name "Jesus," which means "God shall save." By the act of circumcision and by the naming, Jesus was received into the community of Israel, bearing its mark upon his body.

Forty days later, according to Jewish law and custom, Mary and Joseph went to the Temple in Jerusalem for her purification and for the presentation of Jesus in the Temple. After giving birth to a male child, a woman was said to be impure for forty days. Had it been a female baby, Mary would have been impure eighty days! Nevertheless, Mary and Joseph offered two pigeons as a sacrifice. This was the offering of the poor. Had they been wealthier, they would have offered a lamb.

At the same time they presented Jesus at the Temple, dedicating him, as their firstborn, to God. An old man, righteous and devout, Simeon by name, happened to be there when Jesus was presented. Upon seeing the baby Jesus, Simeon was moved to prophesy that this child was destined to change the world. He would bring the redemption of Israel. He would be a light for the Gentiles. Because of him many would rise and many would fall. His presence would expose the secret thoughts of many hearts.

Also at the Temple was an old woman nearly one hundred years old. Her name was Anna and she was a prophetess. She had spent the eight decades of her widowhood at the Temple fasting and praying. Many regarded her words as those of the Lord. Regularly they turned to her for insight into the future and an understanding of the present.

Upon seeing Jesus, Anna, like Simeon, was moved to prophesy that Jesus would bring liberation to Jerusalem. This child is the one we have been expecting. God has blessed you, Mary and Joseph, with a child that will change the world.

Can you imagine the excitement and wonder of Mary and Joseph? Every Jewish mother of that day hoped her newborn son might some day become the Messiah, God's anointed King. Now, at this highly emotional time, Mary and Joseph have been told by two highly respected religious people that their child is to be the one.

There is evidence that Mary and Joseph came to disbelieve these prophecies as the years passed. As life settled into the normal routine, Jesus learned carpentry and spent his life much as any other boy in Nazareth, at least as far as we know. But then things changed. A long hidden flame within the mind and heart of Jesus burst forth. A stirring began within Jesus and Palestine that was to change the world. Joseph probably was dead by that time, but we wonder if Mary remembered what Simeon and Anna had said in the Temple thirty years before. Whether she did or not, we do not know. But that Anna and Simeon were right, we do know. This child changed the world.

And he did so in the ways they predicted.

I

For one thing, *he laid bare the secret thoughts of many.*

Jesus did not have to wait until he was full-grown to do that. It began by calling forth the secret hopes and desires of Simeon and Anna. The child Jesus also brought to consciousness the hopes and aspirations of Mary and Joseph.

The same is true today. The coming of a child into our lives can indeed reveal the secret motives of our hearts. For some girls, getting pregnant is a way to trap a man into marriage. They want not so much a child as a man, and an escape from their present way of life.

For some wives, the opposite is true. They want a child upon whom they can fasten their love and devotion, since they no longer really love their husbands or feel devoted to them. Likewise, the coming of a child can be a threat to a husband, who now finds his wife's attention and affection diverted to the baby. Or the opposite can happen, where a husband pins more hope on his relationship with the child than he does on his relationship with his wife.

Think of the effect of an unwanted child on a family. How it reveals the hidden desires of the heart. What division and animosity it can bring through no fault of its own. The coming of a baby reveals the secret self-concepts parents have. The new life challenges their sense of adequacy, their ability to cope, their easy selfishness and casual freedom. The coming of a baby tells something about the inward heart and its sense of commitment and responsibility.

The coming of a child changes our small personal world and reveals the basic values of our hearts. The ways in which we plan for the new life, the expectations we articulate, the homes we make, and even the kind of talk we use, reveal the secret intents of our hearts. Babies have a way, with all their innocence, of bringing us out into the open. It is not so much that they judge us, as that we judge ourselves by them, as we decide what we will do with them, and how we will react to this new life.

But then, of course, babies grow up. And so it was with Jesus, growing up in wisdom and stature, in favor with God and man. And if by his infancy he revealed the secret thoughts and motives of many, by his manhood he did so even more. John observes he would trust himself to no one, for he knew what was in the hearts of men.

In his own time he laid bare the deceit and hypocrisy so prevalent. Corrupt hearts and vicious motives were brought out of their festering, putrid dungeons to be observed in the high-noon sun of righteousness. The ultimate deceit of doing good things for the wrong reasons was laid bare by this man of fiery integrity. This child grew up to change the world by insisting on truthfulness, openness, integrity, and the pure heart. And wherever this idea is accepted, it still foments change.

Note further that this child changed the world *because he caused the fall of many.*

King Herod was no fool. Politically shrewd as he was, he could sense political danger miles and years away. No wonder he was unsettled when the Wise Men from the East, the astrologers, appeared. He knew it was possible for a newborn child to change the world. After all, how else does it happen? Only Herod wanted to be sure it was his child, not one of some unknown parentage who cared nothing for Herod's name and reputation. Thus, entirely in keeping with his character, he killed all babies of Bethlehem under two years of age. He missed Jesus, of course, and Herod today is remembered only as a backdrop to the story of Jesus. Herod and Augustus Caesar, in all their power, fell, and Jesus, in all his weakness, was exalted.

Jesus caused the fall of many because he spoke the truth of God's prophet. Prophets have a way of leveling the vanity and pretension of corrupt power. Elijah, the great prophet nine centuries before Christ, spoke out against the corruption and idolatry of King Ahab and Queen Jezebel. Eight centuries before Christ, Amos castigated King and High Priest for their corruption and deceit. He warned businessmen and community leaders that their land would be destroyed unless they practiced justice and loved righteousness. But no change took place, and by the power of the Assyrians, Israel was destroyed.

Six centuries before Christ, the prophet Jeremiah warned Judah and Jerusalem that they would be destroyed unless repentance, righteousness, and true faith were practiced in the land. King Zedekiah resented Jeremiah and had him imprisoned. The King complained that Jeremiah never said anything good about him. Jeremiah replied he would be glad to say something good about the King if there was something good to say. Later in history, King Herod hoped John the Baptist would have something good to say about him, but instead he was hotly criticized by the prophet when he attended the prophet's preaching meetings out on the Jordan riverside.

Likewise with Jesus. Not everyone liked what he had to say, because it judged them, criticized them, and revealed their sins. Honey may attract more flies than vinegar, but the prophet of God is constrained to tell the truth. Flattery may get you a long way in building an institution of religion, but the messenger of God is constrained to speak the word of righteousness, even when it means the downfall of many.

Churches and ministers struggle with this principle. How tempting it is always to tell people what they want to hear. How alluring it is to take the spirit of the times, bring it in to the church, sing and pray around it, and baptize it as God's Spirit. The latest intellectual fashion or psychological fad can sound so right and authoritative. Yet, very often the truth of God stands in contradiction of what for the moment seems to be so right, so in, so sophisticated. There are well-known ways for packing them in, but not all ways are true to the gospel.

It has been said by many that if you preach the gospel, people will beat a path to your door to hear you. I don't think that is necessarily so. Big crowds are not necessarily a measure of whether the gospel is being preached. Paul surely preached the gospel more effectively than most, and he did not always attract big crowds. Often it was the opposite, working mostly with small groups. While Jesus had his share of multitudes, he also had large numbers who turned away from him when they learned what discipleship was all about.

Simeon and Anna were right. Many fell away because of Jesus. They could not bear his words of truth. The change he required was too painful. They had wanted him to bless their way of life, rather than change it. Consequently, they fell away, and still do. Many a minister's heart has been broken by those who had come so close and then had turned and walked out of the church because the word spoken did not confirm their prejudice or uphold their corrupt interpretation of life. They were not seeking the truth. They were looking for someone to bless the lies of their lives. The true prophet will never do it. And many will fall away because of it. In that way Jesus was a child who changed the world.

III

Jesus was a child that changed the world because *he caused the rise of many.*

Simeon, old and devout, holding the baby Jesus in his arms in the Jerusalem Temple long ago, was no fool. We would do him a disservice if we regarded him as a sentimental grandfather doting, in his old age, over a baby. He had seen too much of life to do that. He knew the harsh realities of history. Simeon was not waiting around only to indulge in nostalgia or wishful thinking. Wise and perceptive man that he was, he was waiting for the redemption of Israel. He longed for the liberation of Israel, and with mystic insight he saw Jesus as the liberator.

But note this. Jesus was the occasion for Simeon's rise, because Jesus was the one for whom he was looking. Now that he had seen the fulfillment of his hopes, he could die in peace, knowing his life had not been in vain.

Simeon raises an important question for all of us: for what are we looking? What is uppermost in your dreams and longings? What would most satisfy you? What would it take to grant you fulfillment?

Some might answer that they wish they had a husband or wife who really loved them. Others might long for financial success, or fame, or for a chance to change history. Some hope only for a good job, or a new car, or a large inheritance, or an extraordinary vacation.

What do you most want for your children? Good education? Financial success? Good job? Happy marriage? Healthy grandchildren? Well, yes, I suppose most all of us want that. But how many of us long for our children and grandchildren to love God and Jesus Christ? Is the work of Christ's Kingdom uppermost in our minds, or is it only a cultural accessory to the basic way of life we already have chosen?

Who are the people exalted by this child who changed the world? In his own words, he has said the Kingdom belongs to the meek, the merciful, the pure in heart, the peacemakers, the comforters, the seekers after righteousness, the sufferers. The Kingdom belongs to those who humble themselves, who take the less conspicuous seats at banquets, who come to serve rather than to be served, who have hearts and minds seeking after truth and integrity, justice, and love. These are they who will be raised up and exalted.

Not possible, you say. You think the Christ Child is too weak. You believe he is no match for the harsh, brutal, blatant power of the world. You think we have succumbed to sentimentality like Simeon and Anna in the Temple.

No, that is not the case. We believe that the power and Spirit of God is with this child now become man. The Herods and Caesars and Napoleons and Hitlers and Stalins come and go. They have their day. They blossom and flourish like the grass of the field, and then they wither away, die, and are forgotten.

But not the Kingdom of Christ. Year after year, century after century, his Kingdom marches on. In language after language people sing his praises. In structures which range from mud huts to simple, wooden-frame buildings to ornate cathedrals, millions upon millions bend the knee in prayer and adoration to this Child King. His Kingdom marches on, transcending every national boundary, every barrier of time, every atheistic citadel, every intellectual denial — marching on and on into every expectant, receptive heart like those of Simeon and Anna. These are they who are raised up by this child that changed the world.

"He came to his own home, and his own people received him not. But to all who received him, who believed in his name, he gave power to become children of God; who were born, not of blood nor of the will of the flesh nor of the will of man, but of God" (John 1:11-13). There is no greater change that could ever come to the world.

Prayer

Eternal God, who existed before all time, who is present in time, and will continue to exist when time has ceased to be, you have ordained the universe to exist in time and you have, in your providence, set the sun and moon in their places to mark day and night and to measure seasons and festival days. Even in your eternal timelessness you have given us the rhythm of time to measure our days upon earth. We praise and adore you.

We confess before you, O God, our frustration with time — with its swift passage and our squandering of its precious gift. In this holiday season, when many of us remember and mourn our loved ones — with us a few moments in time, then taken from us before their time — when we remember them we confess our propensity to take time for granted and our tendency not to be thankful for each moment we have.

Some of us are frivolous with time. Some of us have too much time on our hands, others of us only mark time or kill time or passively await our time. Forgive any misuse of time, O God, and teach us to number our days and to get a heart of wisdom.

O God, who wishes to make all our time full of meaning, come anew to each of us in this festival season. Open our minds in reverence and awe to the presence of the Christ. Open our hearts to our family and to our beloved. Let grudges of times past be cast aside so that this Christmas can be the first day of the rest of our life. Infuse our weary and burdened spirit with a new gift of your divine energy so that we might, with new zest, work for peace on earth, good will toward men.

We thank you, O God, for all gifts of time, especially for Jesus Christ in whom time was begun, redeemed, and fulfilled. Through Jesus Christ our Lord. Amen.

Words, Words, Words — And The Word

John 1:1-18

One of my favorite cartoons appeared in *The New Yorker* magazine. It showed the building which housed the pressrooms of *The New York Times*. And from the windows of the building oozed words, words, words like streaming waterfalls down into the street to form a flood tide of words, words, words. The cartoonist surely must have decided on his satirical sketch after leafing through the Sunday *Times* for five or six hours. In one proverbial picture worth a thousand proverbial words, the artist commented forcefully on our age of verbal overkill. We have been deluged with words, words, words, written and spoken, loud and soft, stupid and wise, frivolous and poignant.

The deluge of words is well illustrated by the book publishing industry. Prior to the year 1500, Europe was producing books at the rate of about 1,000 titles a year. It took a century to produce a library of 100,000 titles. But by 1950, Europe was producing 120,000 titles, not a century, but a year! By the mid-'60s the world output of books, including that of Europe, was nearly 1,000 titles per day.

If 2,500 years ago the author of Ecclesiastes could sigh, "Of the making of books there is no end, and much study is a weariness of flesh," what would he do in our day of actual mountains of published glut? If, after the initial shock, he were able to avoid complete desperation he would, like us, resign himself to the fact that he never would be able to read all the books that aroused his interest. And upon entering one of our libraries or bookstores, would he not wonder along with us if amidst all these words there might be a word for us, a word of hope, of help, of significant personal meaning?

It is an age of verbal overkill. There is the endless chatter of children, the perpetual pulp of television, the nauseous drone of a jaded teacher, the innocuous harangue of the sales manager, the insidious graspings of ruthless greed cloaked beneath some of the nation's most creative artwork. Television talk shows, lectures, radio talk shows, speeches, trial summations before judge and jury, charge and countercharge, cocktail party chatter, seminars, reports, arguments and debate, the endless drivel of the disc jockey, the pulpit tone drone of sermons. (Did I say sermons? Yes, even sermons!) Talk, talk, talk; words, words, words.

So after our eardrums have been assaulted long enough, after coming to the brink of losing the privacy and control of our inner self, after the nerves have been frazzled again and again by words, words, words, do we not want to breathe deeply, collect our strength, and cry out in the rage of our last reserves of emotional energy, "Is there not a word for us, the word that would put all the other words in perspective to give coherence and meaning"? Six hundred years before Christ, the Judean king, Zedekiah, was seeking the counsel of the prophets of the land, who falsely assured him that God was with him. Yet amidst the babbling of the court prophets, King Zedekiah went secretly to the room where the true prophet, Jeremiah, was imprisoned, asking, "Is there any word from the Lord?"

We too have come aside from all the false prophets of the world, away from all the strident voices of cocksure advice, aside from the rude interruptions of jangling telephones and blatant commercials to ask in the silence, "Is there today, amidst all the words, words, a word from the Lord?" And like Jeremiah, we answer, "Yes, there is a word from the Lord." In fact, the very Word of God himself would speak with us. And he is saying two things: Grace is greater than law, and light is greater than darkness.

I

We've heard the law more times than we like to remember.
We know that in the Law God said,
   "Thou shalt honor thy father and thy mother."

And we said,
   "To hell with my old man
      and my mother is too naive to understand.
   We'll do it our own way,
      because in our day of exploding knowledge,
      pieces of which we all get at college,
   The sons now know more than their fathers
      and daughters are much more well-known
      than their mothers, so they say,
   Gone away to college as they are,
      mini-skirted, maxi-skirted, minus-skirted,
         plus car.
   They are cool,
      and cold, we might as well say it,
      and not play it false,
   Their gain is everyone's loss."

But the Law was repeated,
   "Thou shalt honor thy father and thy mother."

And we said,
   "They live too long
   and know too little,
   for the wiser son's honor or
   active daughter's admiration."

And in the Law God said,
   "Thou shalt not steal."

And we said,
   "Get out there and get it while the getting's good;
   ask questions later;

take or you'll be taken.
And we took and were taken
by our father's brother and
our sister's son, fakin' it,
uncle and nephew, telling nephew and uncle, sorry,
but that's the way it's done in the system, you know.
Your loss is, heh, heh, our gain, no personal offense,
of course,
it's the rules of the game,
of course."

And in the Law God said,
    "Thou shalt not murder."

And we said,
    "It's the furthest thing from our minds,
        about as far away as Vietnam,
        or maybe Afghanistan
    Or our battle plan for attacking the freeway
                at rush hour,
        with three double martinis and a heavy foot.
    Murder has never entered our minds,
        but a man has to unwind
        with a little hate here and there,
    In Greenwich or Haight-Ashbury;
    And it's quite unfair to say that
        longing for his or her death in place of divorce
                is murder,
        or so we said in our tears at the grave."

And in the Law God said,
    "Thou shalt not commit adultery."

And we said,
    "Adultery? What is adultery? Whatever it is,
        everyone's doing it,

said the blue-eyed syphilitic blond,
and the all-American AIDS-stricken boy."

And in the Law God said,
   "Thou shalt not bear false witness."

And we said,
   "If we tell the truth our product may not sell,
      and it would not be well
   to lose our jobs or not pay our bills.
   And so the government passed the laws:
   Truth in packaging, Truth in lending,
   Truth in advertising,
   not, of course, because we're dishonest men,
   goodness knows we wouldn't wrong our neighbor."

And in the Law God said,
   "Thou shalt not covet."

And we said,
   "Of course not, but remember come September,
   we want discontent
   with last year's car, and furniture that's mellowed with
   memories, soiled and sat-in.
   And God said, and my mother said,
   and, said my father, so said my brother.
   The boss said his wife said, and the president said
   what ought to be said when I said I could no longer
   say what ought to be said; but the teacher said
   do not leave off saying when what ought to be said can
   be said with knowledge of the saying.
   And the psychiatrist said that
   what he was saying, was that what I had said was well
   worth saying
   (about $200 an hour). And I said to the preacher
   all I'd been saying, and he said, try praying,
   Then you'll remember this saying, That God said,
   'Thou shalt not....' "

Oh no, no! No more! Woe is me. I am a man of unclean lips. Depart from me, Lord, for I am a sinful man. I have sinned and fallen short of your glory. I am a lawless man, overcome with my iniquity, and my sins are ever before me. Now let me die the death I deserve.

Then the word of the Lord came to me, saying,
"The Word became flesh;
he came to dwell among us,
and we saw *his* glory,
such glory as befits the Father's only Son,
full of grace and truth.
Out of his full store
we have all received grace upon grace;
for while the law was given through Moses,
grace and truth came through Jesus Christ."

II

In the second place, light is greater than darkness.

Some of us talk a lot, not because we have a lot to say. Quite the contrary. We talk excessively in an effort to cover up the fact that we really have nothing to say. Just as Jesus observed that many people like, in their prayers, to impress God with their "much-speaking," so too do they like to impress us.

I remember well a seminary classmate who was afflicted with "running-off-at-the-mouth" disease. Upon encountering him we regularly would receive a massive oration on the latest philosopher or theologian which he had finished reading. When he paused for a breath, we politely would turn to leave for our next class, only to be accompanied down the hall with a continuation of his rapid-fire summary.

It was not that he lacked intelligence. He had plenty of that. Rather, he lacked security. In his endless spate of words there seemed to be no word for him or us. He never came in for a landing, but zoomed off again like a professional tourist who could not bear the thought of staying in one place long enough for his life to catch up with him. He was afraid of finding out who he really was.

66

The fear of discovering the real problem of his true identity was such a threat that he was off and running before an honest-to-God reflective moment could settle in upon him. Such is the problem of many professional students and tourists. They cannot face up to themselves. Their pathological insecurity will not allow them to stop long enough to hear the word *about* them and *for* them.

We see similar patterns in the person who drinks excessively. Instead of words or places, it is drinks. Is it not the same with those involved in the excessive use of tranquilizers or marijuana or barbiturates or cocaine? Are they not devices for flight from the self? Are they not methods of escape from harsh reality? Are they not testimonies to our inadequacy for life? They serve to illustrate the point — that the realities of life seem unbearable, that the fear of death haunts us all.

But we need not stop there. The excessive use of food often signifies the same malaise, as does the obsession with material goods. Many of us discover that at various times in our lives we are little more than sophisticated pack rats. And it matters little whether we pack away lands, houses, money, antiques, or the very best art. Any or all of these *may* be evidences of a deep emptiness, or inner void, or a basic feeling of insignificance for which we must compensate, and indeed, overcompensate.

The rich man by his riches seeks to prove that he is not poor. The compulsive talker seeks to demonstrate that he is not without the word, the truth. The glutton seeks to forestall insecurity, and thereby, symbolically, death. The professional tourist avoids his finiteness, as does the professional student. Existential reality and the threat of death are thus avoided. So too the compulsive worker finds his identity, significance, and self-justification by way of his impressively busy schedule. So too the insecure man who becomes a policeman. Irony of ironies, the insecure man becomes a security officer.

And now a word of caution. Note that we are *not* saying that food, work, money, travel, study, alcohol, drugs, words, culture, or any such things are inherently wrong. It is rather their use by the self to deceive the self so that the self is unable to come to itself, to come clean with itself and God, which is the perversion.

Ah, but such deception, such lying, such darkness. Oh, my friends, this is what the Christ, the Word of God, uncovers and reveals. This is what the author of Hebrews meant when he said, "The word of God is living and active, sharper than any two-edged sword, piercing to the division of soul and spirit, of joints and marrow, and discerning the thoughts and intentions of the heart. And before him no creature is hidden, but all are open and laid bare to the eyes of him with whom we have to do" (Hebrews 4:12-13).

And is this not what John's Gospel means when it says, "The light shines on in the dark, and the darkness has never mastered it." That is the joy of the Gospel, of the Word amidst all our words, that Jesus was not afraid to face up to himself, to the void within, to the question of the meaning of *his* existence.

And since he was true to God and true to himself, he *became* the truth. Since he was able to confess the darkness, God gave him light and made him the light. Acknowledging the ultimate futility of man's words, he received God's Word and became the Word of God for all men. Confessing God's goodness instead of presupposing and defending his own, he became God's good man par excellence. Seeking not to grasp after the status of God, as most men, he humbled himself in faith and obedience so that God grasped and exalted him to the status of divinity. He did not presume upon God by means of genealogical pedigree or cultural-economic status, but yielded instead, without presumption, his faith and allegiance to God.

The deceivers of this world and those being deceived and those deceiving themselves did not receive him and do not even yet. "But to all who did receive him, to those who have yielded him their allegiance, he gave the right to become children of God, not born of any human stock, or by the fleshly desire of a human father, but the offspring of God himself" (John 1:12-13). Light is greater than darkness.

"In the beginning,
The Spirit of God brooded over the icy wastes
       of remote matter which sat there,

sullen-like in the darkness,
    an impregnable cold mass
eternally resistant to penetration —
    or so it seemed,
condemned forever to the void —
    we thought;

Until in the blackness a voice was heard,
    bouncing from eon to eon,
echoing back into light-year spaces,
    with all the graces of a bird in free flight.
Out of the night it came,
    and in a word
'Let there be light' and light became,
never to be overcome by the darkness.
In the beginning-again,
    the New Beginning,
The Spirit of God broods
    over the icy wastes of remote hearts,
    masses of impregnable cold,
        eternally resistant to penetration —
            or so it seems,
    condemned forever to the abyss,
    or so we have been thinking;

Until in the black, desperate void,
    a voice was heard,
    ever so faintly in the deep reaches of the mind,
echoing back along endless corridors
    of forgotten memories and extinguished
        hopes,

saying,
'I am the way, the truth and the life.
He who believes in me shall never die,
    but have life — life everlasting.'

And the light shines on in the darkness,
and the darkness has never mastered it."

And never will.

Prayer

Eternal God, Father of our Lord Jesus Christ, and our Father; out of whose Being have come all light and life, and out of whose eternal presence all time has come to be, we bow humbly before you to acknowledge your holiness and to adore you for wonders and mysteries we perceive but cannot comprehend. So conscious of our frailty and so aware of the brevity of our days, in this holy season we are drawn to you with yearnings beyond the temporal and with longings beyond human satisfaction.

We thank you that through Jesus Christ you have drawn near to us, that your eternal wisdom has focused upon him to give the fullness of meaning to our time, and that your heart of love has suffered through his heart to manifest your grace and truth for our human living. Praise be to you.

With worries over food and families and gifts given and received, we confess our difficulty focusing upon your peace, good will toward men. Help us to be open to you, that you might cleanse us of all unworthy thoughts and fill us with grace and serenity.

O God, who through the life and death and resurrection of Christ has placed infinite value upon human life and living, be pleased to reassure us again of your love and compassion. If doubt and cynicism have gripped our minds and hearts, grant us a breakthrough to new understandings of your designs for our lives. If disease and hardship have weighed heavily upon us, heal us and infuse us with hope for a better day. If family feuds and tensions with friends and associates have made us tense and uneasy, bring us again to compassion and understanding.

Look mercifully upon the world this night, O Lord. If friends and families have difficulty getting along, how much more the nations of the world. We so much long for justice and peace, and so much deplore war and the threat of war. Help us to remove from our own hearts those things which lead to violence, and grant to all nations the wisdom and grace needed for establishing peace on earth, good will to men.

Be close to each of us with our personal needs. We pray comfort for those who mourn, encouragement for those depressed, reconciliation for those estranged, wisdom and help for those overextended financially, rest and refreshment for the weary and overburdened, and a new measure of grace and love for us all. In Christ's name we pray. Amen.

The Moral Compass

Mark 1:4-11

"Confession is good for the soul," so we say in Lent. And so we say in Advent too, "Confession is good for the soul." And my confession is this. Like many men I hesitate to stop to ask for directions. So much so that my wife presented me with a t-shirt which, on the front, had emblazoned these words: "Real men don't ask directions."

We "real men" like to solve problems on our own. We tend to dislike the feeling of dependency and helplessness implied by asking directions. We like to think we know where we're going, thank you, know as much where we're going as anyone else, thank you! We are sufficient to the task at hand. We can find our way through the corporate jungle, negotiate our path through social and cultural labyrinths, and clear a path through the Byzantine worlds of academia, politics, and club memberships. Weakness, uncertainty, and dependency are not for us. "Real men don't ask directions."

Except when we are in real trouble. Any pilot or navigator or sailor knows that. And my daughters who used to sail with me in their younger days know that. They still talk about an adventure in the fog, all day on Lake Michigan, fifty miles in the fog where we could scarcely see a few feet in front of the boat. And then, after a long, long day of seeing nothing, they saw it — the lighthouse at the end of the channel leading to the safe harbor and the fulfillment of my promise of a nice dinner at a restaurant.

My daughters' faith in me as a sailor and navigator rose significantly in that episode because out of the thick, thick fog I had

73

brought them safely to harbor, right on target, the lighthouse directly in front of us and the sumptuous dinner soon behind it.

Had I asked directions? Indeed I had. Not from anyone on shore, but from my chart of those waters, and from my compass, which was extremely accurate. (That was before I had Loran and GPS!) Any sailor will tell you there is nothing more disorienting than fog. In a thick fog, most people lose whatever innate sense of direction they have. Light is refracted in strange ways. The direction sound is coming from can be deceiving. Any sailor knows that in a thick fog, it is extremely difficult to sail, as we say, "by the seat of our pants." We need at least an accurate chart and an accurate compass.

If that is true in sailing on Lake Michigan or Long Island Sound, it is ever more true sailing on the sea of life. We need an accurate spiritual chart and moral compass. And if on days which seem to be spiritually and morally clear we feel we can sail the sea of life "by the seat of our pants," we will be in desperate trouble in times of spiritual obfuscation and moral confusion.

And it is my conviction we live in such a time — a time of spiritual degeneration and moral confusion, a time of casual cynicism and comfortable skepticism; a time of refined greed and not-so-refined litigiousness, a time of frenzied competitiveness from fear of being left behind, and a time of easily compromised values and equivocated beliefs for the sake of attaining immediate gratification and instant success.

But the hopeful good news is this: we do have a reliable spiritual chart and a stalwart, accurate compass which have given people direction through moral and spiritual fog for centuries. I speak of that remarkable figure of our text — John the Baptist — John the Baptizer, that lonely, rustic, fiery prophet of the Judean wilderness whose voice echoed down the first century Jordan River Valley, rolling down the centuries into the stone and glass canyons of Manhattan Island and across the pleasant estates and waters of Long Island and on across the country — John the Baptist — a moral compass for all time.

And here are his moral directions for our time — repentance and righteousness.

I

Consider first *repentance*. John thunders forth, "Repent, for the Kingdom of Heaven is at hand." John was "preaching a baptism of repentance."

The word "repent" in the Greek language of the New Testament is *metanoia*, which literally means "a change of mind." And not only a change of mind, but a change of direction. It means to turn around, to go the other way. It means not only to feel bad about the direction your life has been taking, but to get a new mind, and to do something about it, to actually change directions.

Probably one of the most disheartening and yet humorous things we hear when we do finally stop to ask for directions is to be told, "You can't get there from here." But when we hear the words of John the Baptist, he is in effect saying, "Yes, you can get there from here." Yes, you can get a new mind. Yes, you can change directions. Yes, you can prepare yourself for the coming of the Kingdom of God.

And one way to do it is to do as John did — go into the wilderness to be alone, to seek solitude, and to listen for the voice of God. I suspect many of us today do not clearly hear the Word of God because we are afraid to hear it. We are afraid to be alone with ourselves, afraid of quietness, afraid of solitude. The cacophony of voices competes for our attention. We are flooded with the inanity of television, with the banalities of movies where human life is trivialized by repeated violence and by sexuality divorced from authentic personhood.

But if you are in a time of moral confusion and personal uncertainty, look for quietness and solitude in the dimensions of worship and study and prayer so as to hear the still, small voice of God. Sailors will tell you, and so will pilots, that when you are in a fog, when it is dark, when you have lost your landmarks and lost certainty of your course, you *must* trust your instruments to guide you through.

There are those among us who live by public opinion polls. Politicians must have them, of course. And smart businesses can make use of them, and even churches. But reliable spiritual and

75

moral directions are seldom found in the herd instinct or mob reaction. On a boat in the fog, you do not take a vote among the crew as to which way to turn. You must trust your instruments.

The true compass for moral and spiritual navigation is to be found with God's prophets — prophets like Elijah and Jeremiah, Amos and Isaiah, and yes, John the Baptist. Usually they are lonely, ostracized, ignored, persecuted, rebuffed, laughed at, and repudiated. But the centuries have proved them right and the majority of us wrong, for they continue to speak while their detractors have long since perished and been forgotten.

John's advice to repent is hopeful good news, because it is something we all can do. John will not accept a blind determinism or an easy acquiescence to fate, or an irresponsible shrug of the shoulders which says my heredity and environment made me this way.

The good news about repentance is that we can change, we can make a new life, we can become a new person, we can do things differently, we can break these addictions, we can avoid the path of destruction, we can improve the self and our relationships, we can change our job, alter our career, change our thinking.

But many of us paint ourselves into a corner and refuse to consider alternatives. In the many years that I have been counseling people in troubled marriages, I have come to the conviction that in at least sixty or seventy percent of the cases, partners can make the needed changes to lead to a happier marriage if they want to. They do not have to repeat the destructive patterns of their past. If they have the ability to recognize the problem, they also have the ability to do something about it.

Each of us knows in his or her own heart the changes that are needed for the better self, the better marriage, the better career, the better citizenship, the better churchmanship, the better parent, the better son or daughter, the better boss, the better employee.

"Repent, for the kingdom of heaven is at hand." That is the good news — we can have a change of mind and heart for a new way of living. Listen in the solitude of spiritual earnestness for the still, small voice of God to guide you. It is the spiritual moral compass.

If John speaks of *repentance*, in Matthew's expanded version of our text, he also proclaims the need for *righteousness*.

"Who warned you to flee from the wrath to come?" he thundered against the public leaders of his time. And then he boldly challenges them, "Bear fruit that befits repentance, and do not presume to say to yourselves, 'We have Abraham as our father'; for I tell you, God is able from those stones to raise up children to Abraham." And then with piercing eyes and authoritative voice he adds, "Even now the axe is laid to the root of the trees; every tree therefore that does not bear fruit is cut down and thrown into the fire" (Matthew 3:8-10).

If individuals are spiritually confused, existing in a moral fog, so are groups and nations — especially our nation. But many people are slow to realize it. I remember only a few years ago a stalwart woman member of our church who proudly proclaimed America as the closest thing to the Kingdom of God on earth. But is it really?

Veterans of World War I wanted to make the world safe for democracy — especially our democracy. Veterans of World War II wanted to fight the war to end all wars and come home to white picket fences and flourishing churches and an age of unprecedented faith in America. Korean War veterans somewhat grudgingly went dutifully to their "police action," and Vietnam veterans confusedly, bitterly, and dutifully went to have their lives wasted.

And the '60s generation marched and protested against their parents' prosperity and pride in what they regarded as the closest thing to the Kingdom of God on earth, and drugged their way in and out of the Woodstocks and free love communes and back-to-earth impulses of eros, long suppressed yet now in full flower; only to be followed by the "me generation," to be succeeded by the greed and impatient selfishness of the "me-right-now generation." Is this beloved country of ours the closest thing there is to the Kingdom of God? Can we claim, "We have Abraham as our father," meaning we have a great past and can rest on our laurels?

I think John the Baptist would choke on his locusts and wild honey at the thought. For example, cheating in our schools has reached an all-time high. And our public education system, despite massive increases in budgets, has declined in educational achievement. William Bennett tells of Judith Kahn, a math teacher at James Madison High School in Brooklyn, who says she loves teaching there because of the immigrants. "They have a drive in them that we no longer seem to have."

At Williams College in the Berkshires, a sociology professor says that Americans have become the object of ridicule among immigrant students on campus. He says, "When immigrant kids criticize each other for getting lazy or loose, they say, 'You're becoming American.'"

A *Washington Post* article told the story of Paulina, a Polish high school student studying in the United States. In Warsaw, she would talk to friends a while after school, go home and eat with her parents, and then do four or five hours of homework. But, says Paulina, "When I first came here, it was like going into a crazy world, but now I am getting used to it. I'm going to Pizza Hut and watching TV and doing less work in school." Then she adds prophetically, "I can tell it is not a good thing to get used to." The Kingdom of God will not come to a people intellectually lazy and morally corrupted.

Nor will it come to a people who have lost moral backbone in the midst of unprecedented affluence. We are a rich and proud and powerful country. There are noble qualities in our nation. But there is a lot that is ignoble. Best-selling novelist John Updike put it this way, "The fact ... that we still live well cannot ease the pain of feeling that we no longer live nobly."

Since 1960, our population has increased 41 percent. Our gross domestic product almost tripled, and total social spending at all levels of government increased nearly five times. However, said William Bennett in a recent speech, "During the same thirty-year period, there was a 560 percent increase in violent crime; more than a 400 percent increase in illegitimate births; a quadrupling in divorces; a tripling of children living in single-parent homes; more than a 200 percent increase in the teenage suicide rate; and a drop of 75 points in the average SAT scores of high school students."

Mr. Bennett goes on to recite these alarming facts: "Today, thirty percent of all births and 68 percent of black births are illegitimate. By the end of the decade, according to the most reliable projections, forty percent of all American births and eighty percent of minority births will occur out of wedlock."

Are things getting worse? Mr. Bennett goes on to compare 1940 student bodies with 1990 student bodies. When in 1940 teachers were asked to identify the top problems in schools, they mentioned chewing gum, talking out of turn, making noise, running in the hall, cutting in line, dress code infractions, and loitering. But guess what teachers said in 1990? They spoke of the top problems being drug use, alcohol abuse, pregnancy, suicide, rape, robbery, and assault. Is it any wonder that many teachers I talk to can hardly wait to retire?

Add to that our increasing atrocity overload where we lose our capacity for shock, outrage, and disgust. We are, says Senator Daniel Patrick Moynihan, "defining deviancy down," and we seem to think the more we can tolerate violence, crime, suicide, substance abuse, and sexual degradation, the more "sophisticated" we are. Our television talk shows feature topics such as cross-dressing couples, women who can't say no to cheating, prostitutes who love their jobs, a three-way love affair, a former drug dealer, and on and on. So in our cities of gold and alabaster, we seem to have moral rot and spiritual corruption at the core, and seventy percent of our populace does in fact admit we are off track.

What should we do? We should follow the example of black leader Delores Tucker, who is fighting the pornographic, violent, misogynistic lyrics of "gangsta" rap. At a Washington civil rights church meeting, emcee Eleanor Norton said, "We (black women) were astonished to hear this filthy, lowdown music, and it was about us." Then she added, "And we looked to the right and looked to the left, and there was silence — until one woman said something and did something."

And that woman was Delores Tucker, who bought stock in Nobody Beats the Wiz, Musicland, Sony, and Time Warner in order to protest at stockholder meetings. This is precisely what she did at the Time Warner stockholder meeting — standing up and reading the unbelievable "gangsta" rap lyrics. Why do the corporations do it? "It's greed-driven, drug-driven, and race-driven," says Tucker.

Tucker, a minister's daughter and former church organist and choir director, says she is motivated by "a passionate love affair for God and my people." Then she adds that in order to make a difference in the world, "I realize we always started at the church and marched to the political kingdom, whether it's local or national," to make a difference. In the meantime, many Christians are totally anemic or naive or spineless when it comes to making a difference.

And what should we do?

Another John the Baptist of our time, William Bennett, who knows the political process well, and notes its importance, says the problem is not primarily political. It is primarily spiritual and moral. It is, he says, *acedia*, a Greek word meaning sloth, yes, but also a negation of and aversion to spiritual things. It manifests itself in a "joyless, ill-tempered, and self-seeking rejection of the nobility of the children of God."

Therefore, more than ever we need a spiritual chart and moral compass to direct us in the way of wholeness and health. And the hopeful good news is that we have them — in the Bible, in the great prophets like Elijah and Amos and John, and of course, in Jesus himself, who like John insisted on repentance and the works of righteousness.

Yes, we self-made, prideful, materialistic, successful American men and women need to confess that it is time to stop and ask for directions. And the hopeful, good news is, we *can* get there from here.

Prayer
Almighty God, by whose power the universe is shaped, and by whose presence all the worlds are sustained, your Mind structures all things, animate or inanimate, and your Spirit infuses the world with the pulse of life. We praise you as participants in the miracle of being, and thank you for consciousness to know you.

We come into your holy presence first to acknowledge we have not lived up to your expectations of us. We easily are distracted from the vision of our higher selves. Our loftiest ideals too quickly are compromised in the pressures of the moment. The noble, courageous things we intended to say, but didn't; the good we had hoped to do, but failed to do; the kindness we should have shown, but neglected — all come to mind in your radiant presence. We confess we are sinners more often by what we fail to do, than by what we have done. Forgive us, O God, and grant us new resolve to become the persons we should become.

If we make our confessions in your holy presence, so also would we make our petitions. We pray especially for people who have lost their way — lost sons and daughters, far from their parents' love in a strange and foreign place; lost husbands or wives, lured from the bonds of faithful commitment to the enticements borne of imagination and infatuation; lost talents in young people who vainly pursue the life of indolence and indifference; lost older people suffocating in the stuffiness of outdated ideas and worn-out memories; lost geniuses who have dissipated their gifts on trivialities; lost disciples of your cause who have succumbed to a hardened skepticism and casual cynicism; lost children, alone and afraid in an adult world often indifferent, neglectful, and violent.

O God, whose nature it is to seek and to save the lost, come to us, wherever we may be on the ways of life, and rescue us from our worst selves, and bring us back, like lost sheep and lost sons and daughters, into the glory of your loving guidance and care. Through Jesus Christ our Lord. Amen.

Religion
Without Guile

John 1:43-51

It was one of those delightful stories out of the American Frontier. Many Easterners are unaware of the formative influences of the American Frontier as chronicled in the writings of many historians, especially those of Frederick Jackson Turner. Very often immigrants to the eastern part of the country clustered first in the ghetto, and then with mastery of English or new skills, gradually moved out of the ghetto and sometimes to the suburbs — but often not "Out West" — meaning anything west of the Hudson River. Chicago was out there somewhere and not far beyond it lay San Francisco. And in between were mostly cowboys and Indians, sod huts and American Gothic farmers.

The classic magazine cover of *The New Yorker* depicting the average New Yorker's vision of America said it beautifully. Beyond the Hudson was Chicago, and in the distance a skyscraper of San Francisco, with little in between!

But for most Americans the frontier was a formative influence. Leaving behind the support of one's own group, advancing into vast spaces and developing a strong sense of self-reliance and independence, coupled with a radical egalitarianism, many Americans owe much to the "frontier experience."

That was also true in religion. Many had left behind particular denominations of their "old world" country. The denominational divisions of the past, often based on national, ethnic, linguistic, and regional rivalries, seemed irrelevant in the vast regions of the new world frontier. But religion itself was not irrelevant. Instead, America was greatly influenced by the Great Awakening of the

1700s led by Congregationalism's Jonathan Edwards and Methodism's George Whitefield.

And in the 1800s, revivalism swept across all of America — from Brooklyn on to the far reaches of the Midwest and West. Religious revivals and theological debates abounded. Religious enthusiasm and intellectual inquiry seemed to go hand in hand.

One delightful story comes out of the American Midwest of the early 1800s. One man, called to enter the ministry, prepared himself with the requisite philosophical, Biblical, historical, and theological studies. The time came for him to be ordained. And after he had presented his required theological position paper, the austere ordination committee interrogated him intensely.

They especially wanted to know more about his views on the Trinity — the Father, Son, and Holy Spirit. They were unclear about his beliefs and wanted him to be more specific and precise.

The ministerial candidate was in a dilemma, because he knew his views on the Trinity did not agree with the orthodox teachings of that denomination. He knew that if he spoke somewhat ambiguously and abstractly, embroidering here and there, he might be able to pass the examination. On the other hand, he knew if he told them what he really believed, they would disqualify him for the ministry.

This was his dilemma. Should he tell a lie and be ordained, or should he tell the truth and be kicked out? He chose the latter, and was indeed kicked out. He decided upon a religion without guile, a religion without deceit or hypocrisy, a religion without deception or falsehood. He opted to stand by his convictions of truth and be rejected, rather than falsifying his beliefs for the sake of acceptance. (By the way, he was later ordained in a denomination which espoused more intellectual liberty.)

Most all of us, in one way or another, have faced similar dilemmas. Should we tell the truth and be kicked out, or support the lie and remain in? Should we express our doubts openly and risk censure, or just cross our fingers when we say the creeds and remain approved? Should we blow the whistle on fraud and deception in religion or business, government or profession? Or should we just go along with the corruption everyone knows about so as not to disturb the status quo? And should we not, of all things, expect religion to be without guile? Of course we should.

I

A religion without guile will have the *courage to stand for the truth*.

That may be what attracted Jesus to Nathanael, a man he described as an Israelite with no guile, no deceit or fraud or hypocrisy. Only John's Gospel mentions Nathanael, whose name means "gift of God." And at first glance, Nathanael comes off as a bit of a snob.

When asked by Philip to come meet Jesus of Nazareth, whom they believed was the Messiah, Nathanael scoffed with the bias of his fellow citizens of Cana (a rival city of Nazareth), saying, "Can anything good come out of Nazareth?" And rather than argue with Nathanael, Philip merely replies, "Come and see."

The other officially religious people of his time, as depicted by John's Gospel, were not nearly as ready to explore new truth. Content in their traditions and self-righteous in their conclusions, they presumed they knew all the essential truth. So they were not receptive to Jesus or his teachings. But Nathanael was — an Israelite in whom there was no self-justifying deceptiveness, no guile.

Jesus saw Nathanael sitting under the fig tree — a place where rabbis and others often sat to study, to meditate, to pray for the messianic age, and to teach. With divine intuition, Jesus perceives him to be a seeker, a man open to new truth, a person willing to face the future with the courage of his convictions. Rather than perpetuate the fraud of commonly accepted lies and delusions, Nathanael had courage to move on to new truths and convictions.

Charles Krauthammer, a popular author and essayist for *Time* magazine, wrote recently of his experience upon being admitted to the hospital. After the usual questions in the admitting office, he was asked his religious preference. Of course, the hospital wanted to know whether to call a minister, priest, rabbi, or mullah in case of emergency, said Krauthammer. But it struck him that many people think of religion in that way — as a matter of preference rather than conviction, as a matter of personal taste rather than eternal value or meaning.

Do you like your coffee black or with milk or cream? Would you like sugar? Do your prefer your eggs scrambled or over easy? Would you like home fries or French fries? Do you prefer Islam, Judaism, or Christianity? It's a matter of consumer taste, bemoaned Krauthammer.

More than that, in our secular culture, tolerance abounds *except* for anyone who is openly and sincerely religious, says Krauthammer. In a democratic society all kinds of political arguments are acceptable, *except* those based in sincere faith. "Call on Timothy Leary or Chairman Mao, fine. Call on Saint Paul, and all hell breaks loose," said Krauthammer. (*Time*, June 15, 1998, p. 92)

Yale University Law School professor, Dr. Stephen Carter, lamented much the same in his book, *The Culture of Disbelief.* He says much of contemporary secular culture treats religion as if it were a mere consumer choice, a mere matter of private preference and personal taste. God is treated more or less as a personal hobby, and religion is an activity of personal preference, which has little or nothing to do with public life and behavior.

In our secular culture, "Taking religion seriously," says Professor Carter, "is something only those wild-eyed zealots do ..." (p. 24). In other words, sincerely religious people are an implied threat to the prevailing authorities and accepted truths and politically correct dogmas. Sincerely religious people, believing in a transcendent reality, are always open to a new way of seeing which may severely threaten the accepted way of seeing. As Dr. Carter puts it, "A religion is at its heart a way of denying the authority of the rest of the world" (*op. cit.,* p. 41).

Jesus admired Nathanael as a man of courageous faith in whom there was no fraud, no cringing acquiescence to the political correctness police of the left or right, no unthinking groveling before the herd psychology or mob instinct, no rigid, opinionated, agnostic cynic who was too lazy to read new challenges to his thought.

No, here was a man who responded to Philip's invitation to "come and see." And Nathanael went and saw and believed, and so must we, if our religion is to be without guile.

II

A religion without guile will also *affect morals and ethics and behavior*. A religion without guile will practice what it preaches.

I am reminded of a Mexican bandit who robbed a Laredo, Texas, bank and was apprehended on a busy street by a U.S. marshal a few days later.

The marshal spoke no Spanish and the Mexican spoke no English, so a passing Mexican was asked to be the interpreter. The marshal poked a gun in the bandit's belly and said to the interpreter, "Ask him if his name is Gonzales." The interpreter said, "He says, si, he is Manuel Gonzales." "Ask him if he was in Laredo at the First National Bank." The interpreter said, "He says he was and he admits he robbed the bank."

The marshal pushed the gun further into the bandit's belly. "Now tell him I'm going to pull the trigger if he doesn't tell me where the money is." With sweat pouring down his face the thief stammered in Spanish, "Don't shoot! I got a wife and four kids at home. The money is in the well behind the house."

The interpreter said to the marshal, "He says you one big mouth. You no scare him. Go ahead and shoot!" When it comes to applying our religion to our ethics and behavior, many of us are like that interpreter!

Some of Jesus' harshest criticism was of those whose religious beliefs did not make a difference in their practice. And while we might expect promises and performance to be contradictory in politicians, it is especially odious when religious leaders violate the essential teachings of their religion.

Consider, for example, the recent indictment by state and federal authorities of the minister who is the President of the National Baptist Convention, USA. Reverend Henry Lyons has been named in 56 counts including extortion, fraud, and tax evasion. Federal authorities claim he cheated corporations out of five million dollars, to purchase cars, jewelry, trips, country club memberships, and a Florida beachfront house for his alleged mistress. If convicted, Reverend Lyons could be sentenced to a maximum of 815 years in prison and 25 million dollars in fines. If the charges are true, Reverend Lyons is a blatant contradiction of the religion he espouses.

The late Christopher Lasch once asked what accounted for our society's wholesale defection "from the standards of personal conduct — civility, industry, self-restraint — that were considered indispensable to democracy." His answer was the "decay of religion." Religion, he observed, had come to be a matter of indifference to many and was left out of public debate. It became less and less relevant to public behavior (quoted in Robert Bork, *Slouching Towards Gomorrah*, p. 274).

While many Americans — over ninety percent — say they believe in God, and while nearly half say they pray every day, and while forty percent say they attend religious services once a week — while many profess belief, it often does not follow through in ethical behavior.

Indeed, many religious people — especially from the right — are suspect if they enter the public arena with religious convictions. But historically speaking, the American Revolution, the abolition of slavery, women's suffrage, the temperance movement, on down to the civil rights movement led by Martin Luther King, Jr. — all these political movements for freedom, equality, justice, and ethics had a strong religious core and emphasis. Indeed, the Great Awakening of the eighteenth century and the Revivalism of the nineteenth century often fueled these great social reformations.

A religion without guile will not only *talk* of freedom and justice and equality, it will *act* for them. A religion without guile will not only preach against corruption in business and government, it will advocate publicly for honesty. A religion without guile will not just be a privatized, personalized activity of consumer taste; it will be a bastion of conviction against all the insidious power which would exploit our true humanity.

Jesus, at the beginning of his ministry, said of Nathanael, "Behold an Israelite without guile," because he was willing to "come and see" to enter the frontier of new truth.

However, we don't hear much about Nathanael again until the very last chapter of John's Gospel, where after Jesus' death Nathanael goes fishing on the Sea of Galilee with some of the other disciples. It was there, after the resurrection, that Nathanael and the others experienced yet another frontier — the presence of the Risen Christ in their breakfast on the beach.

After their miraculous catch of fish they came to shore. And the risen Jesus was there, beside a charcoal fire on the beach, with fish being cooked on it. "Come and have breakfast," he invited them.

And they did. And Nathanael saw the glory of the Son of Man — now manifested in the Risen One — the glory promised when first he believed. He saw and believed and acted because his was a religion without guile.

Prayer

Almighty God, who has created the universe in majesty and mystery, and who has brought forth humanity in your image to manifest your love and glory, we thank you for all the wonders we behold and the opportunities we have been given. All life and living is a gift from you. We give you thanks and praise.

We come before you, O God, for a cleansing of the soul. Jesus has promised, "Blessed are the pure in heart, for they shall see God." So we come to you for purity of heart. Help us always to come to the truth about ourselves and our relationships. Give us clarity and insight so we might be rid of self-deception and be cleansed of lingering guilt. Save us from self-rationalization and self-justification which fortify the self against coming clean with you. Cleanse our hearts of all unrighteousness and forgive our sins, that we might behold you in all your beauty and purity.

We pray for our church and the Church throughout the world. Strengthen us to act with purer motive and to do with good conscience the works of righteousness of your Kingdom. Keep us from falsehood, from deceit and arrogance. Grant that with integrity we might be the salt of the earth and the light of the world. Strengthen and bless your Church with purity of heart and a renewed faith from a vision of your holiness. Through Jesus Christ our Lord. Amen.

Academics, Fanatics, And Other Disciples

Mark 1:14-20

I must confess that I am not much of a fisherman. Over the years I have tried my hand at fishing, but the Izaak Walton League would be sure to look the other way if I applied for membership.

To be sure, growing up in Wisconsin I did try my luck at some of those beautiful trout streams. But you would have been unwise to wait with a hearty appetite while I tried to catch our dinner. And, yes, my friends and I did go fishing on the nearby Mississippi River. And, yes, we did throw in a line from time to time, but at that age — our teenage years — we were far more interested in racing our motorboats up and down the river and jumping the wake of the huge barges and tugboats.

I was not much of a fisherman nor was I the son of a fisherman. But my daughters were a different story, especially when they were quite young. While vacationing on a lake in northern Michigan, I would take them out in the boat to a well-known spot to fish for bass. I would help them bait their hooks. They would throw in their lines, and almost before I got my line in the water, they were hauling in bass. One after another they would reel them in with gleeful excitement. And on my fishing line — nothing, zero! Now and then I will still drop a line off my sailboat, but with no success. I admit it. I was not and am not much of a fisherman.

But Peter, Andrew, James, and John were a different matter. Living on the shores of the Lake of Galilee, they with their fathers were professional, commercial fishermen. This small, oval-shaped lake, twelve by seven miles, had long been an important source of fish not only for Palestine, but for export to places as distant as Rome. The Jewish historian Josephus tells us that in his time (shortly after Christ) at least 130 fishing boats sailed Galilee. Their catches were salted and sent everywhere as a staple in their diets.

While Peter, Andrew, James, and John were not wealthy, they were not poor either. Apparently successful in their businesses, they owned their own boats and used hired help to expand their operation. Like most fishermen, they knew the importance of timing, location, bait, and patience. And like many fishermen, they no doubt had a kind of mystical appreciation of the sea and the weather and all the world of nature.

It was while these successful fishermen were mending their nets on the seashore that Jesus, the ex-carpenter and would-be leader of men, approached them. "Follow me," he said directly and dramatically, "and I will make you fishers of men." So they left their fathers, their boats and nets, and the hired help and followed him.

Such was the beginning of Jesus' ministry — changing fishermen into fishers of men, converting businessmen who fed people physically to kingdom men who fed people spiritually. They left an occupation to respond to a vocation — a calling. Instead of luring fish into their nets, Jesus lured them into luring people to join in their cause. In place of the comfortable, settled, bourgeois life of Palestine, they were challenged to the uncertainties of campaigning for the Messianic Age, for the Kingdom of God Jesus was announcing.

And ever since Jesus has been calling disciples to his cause, luring men and women away from mere occupation to vocation, enlisting them in a spiritual army to do battle with evil, calling them away from the settled, comfortable life to the high seas of adventure, boldly announcing they were out to the change the world.

Over the centuries there have been many kinds of disciples. But today let us consider at least two types which must be held in balance — academics and fanatics.

I

Let's consider *fanatics* first.

It must be admitted that the word "fanatic" does not have a popular ring to it. It conjures images of wild-eyed, frenzied commitment to a cause, no questions asked. It suggests unswerving devotion, unquestioning allegiance, and fierce loyalty. No alternatives are considered. For the fanatic, his way is the *one, right* way. And when joined to the word "religious," the notion of religious fanatic breeds a negative reaction in most of us.

However, when we use the shortened version of fanatic, the word is softer and more acceptable. And what is the shortened version? The word "fan," as in sports fan or race fan or fan club. A fan club is literally a club of fanatics, which seems to be entirely acceptable when attached to sports heroes, celebrities, or rock music stars. Political fanatics are much less acceptable and religious fanatics least acceptable of all.

A man in one church recalled how during football season he and his son watched football on television the whole weekend. On Saturdays it was college football, on Sundays professional football, and then to cap it off professional football on Monday evenings.

This same father was uncomfortable with his son being away for a weekend religious retreat, fearing his son might turn into a religious fanatic! I asked him if he thought being a sports fan was okay for his son. Of course, he replied. But when I pointed out that "fan" is the shortened form of "fanatic," he was taken aback.

His long-neglected wife, a football widow of the first rank, wondered aloud why it was perfectly acceptable to be a football fanatic and not a religious fanatic. "Because," replied her husband without thinking, "unlike a religious fanatic, a football fanatic can be perfectly harmless." "Yes," said the long-unnoticed football widow, "I can vouch for that!"

Nevertheless, we are rightly concerned about religious fanaticism — a religious devotion and fervor which refuses to admit any questions or to raise any doubts. History is replete with atrocities committed in the name of religion. Think of the ancient religions of Mexico and Central America where virgin girls were sacrificed to ensure the rising of the sun. Or consider the sacrifice of sons and daughters in the ancient Near East to appease angry gods. Or recall the mass suicide of the Jimmy Jones devotees in Guyana a few years ago. Or think of the Ayatollah Khomeni enlisting children and young people to run through Iraqi minefields, promising them immediate entrance into paradise.

Of course, the questioning can go on and on. One man's convictions are another man's fanaticism. But, we ask, what about religions that refuse blood transfusions or the use of doctors or medicine, or religions that keep women and minorities as second-class persons, or religions that endorse caste and class and corrupt political establishments? Think of wars fought as holy wars, vicious wars in the name of God. Even the holy wars of the Bible where *herem* or holocaust was practiced, which meant the complete destruction of all men, women, children, cattle, and possessions of the enemy. History is replete with the devoted, destructive fervor of religious fanatics.

That is why Jesus called *disciples* to himself, not fanatics. The word "disciple" means "learning follower." Therefore, a disciple is not just one who blindly follows a leader, but one who learns as he or she follows. Common in the ancient world, great teachers like Socrates, Plato, and Aristotle gathered disciples about them who both followed and learned. And in the manner of Jewish rabbis of the time, Jesus gathered disciples, or learning followers, around him. It is interesting to note that his disciples most often called him rabbi, or teacher, or master. Learning was a part of discipleship.

Many Christians have suffered tremendously on this side of the equation. What following of Jesus we have done has not been well thought-out. Once our children are confirmed, we rarely see them again. For some strange reason we have felt our educational task was complete. So we send them off to college with at best a second or third grade religious education and then wonder why they fall away from the faith.

In many churches adult education is almost nonexistent. Many adults have not seriously opened a Bible or mature book of theology in years. And if we do read devotional books they often are the pabulum type written by the likes of Roy Rogers and Trigger!

94

Ours is not a fanaticism of devotion but of indifference. Our fanaticism is not a flagrant fervor of authoritarian self-righteousness, but a studied avoidance of any religious commitment at all. When Jesus comes close to us in our occupations we tend to cling tighter and tighter to the boats and nets rather than take the risk of leaving them. Fearful of fanaticism, we founder on nihilism — nothingism.

Jesus said the two great commandments summed up all religion. The first great commandment is to love the Lord our God with all our heart, soul, strength, and *mind*. Unthinking discipleship will not do. A lazy mind and indolent brain are not what Jesus had in mind when he called people toward God. Why is it, he might ask, that Christians believe they must check their minds and intelligence at the door of the church?

In many parts of the world people are participating in the knowledge explosion. However, at the same time many Christians are experiencing a knowledge fizzle. We want a Reader's Digest Bible where Adam and Eve goofed, Noah cruised on a rainy weekend, and God gave two or three suggestions.

Ignorance will not lead the world of tomorrow, nor will fanatic devotion to memories of faded realities. If we Christians are going to stop retreating from the world with our tail between our legs, and turn around and lead, we are going to have to get smart. We are going to have to get a "thinking man's" religion again, to love God with our minds as well as our emotions and sentiments.

To be sure, true religion has to do with the heart, with the feelings and emotions, with, as Pascal said, the reasons of the heart, which the mind (that is, the cold, rational mind) knows not of. To be sure, religion has to do with the soul, the will, the inmost decision-making center of the self. And, yes, it has to do with strength, with energy and action.

But to all fanatics, to all authoritarian religions convinced God is in their box and possessed by their religious system, to all true believers who never doubt their views, Jesus might say in the words of Oliver Cromwell, "I beseech you brethren, by the mercies of God, think it possible you might be mistaken."

Yes, Jesus calls us to discipleship — thinking, learning discipleship accompanied by devotion and energy.

II

If some of Jesus' disciples have tended to be fanatics, others have tended to be *academics*.

I must confess that I have a definite sympathy for this kind of discipleship. My world has long been the world of classrooms, libraries, lecture halls, and seminars. After spending four years in college and six years in graduate schools with four earned degrees, I find my life still resonates to the rhythm of the academic calendar. Each fall the college campus has a certain allure for me. And when the snow falls, I can be very content in the library or seminar room. Adventures of the mind have always excited me.

The same is true of the life with books and magazines. My study is lined with packed bookshelves and stacks of books on credenza and tables. And my study and bedrooms at home are full of magazines and books. My wife shudders each time we pass a bookstore!

And yet, for all my love of the life of the mind, Jesus' call for discipleship is more than a call for scholarship. Jesus did not command his disciples to be just thinkers, but to be lovers — and loving is an activity more inclusive than thinking. Just think of the devastation and destruction brought upon the world by great thinkers who were not great lovers. We now are challenged to use our great thinking to love the earth and our fellow humans rather than destroy them with weapons, technology, and pollution.

But perhaps the greatest weakness of the academic disciple is not evil action but the triple *A*'s of academia — aloofness, abstruseness, and abstraction. Obsessed with the notion of pure thought and pure science, the academic disciple never comes down to earth to sully his or her hands with the harsh realities of daily life.

The academic type disciple is a modern-day gnostic or dualist who believes God is known through thought more than action. If God is pure Mind, they reason, then one can get closest to God by thinking his thoughts after him. God is best known, they argue, in the latest thoughts of the leading colleges, universities, and authors.

Thus, the academic world becomes the Holy of Holies of the modern world wherein one enters with a 4.0 GPA and the highest SAT scores and the best recommendations and essays. Ours is, therefore, salvation by knowledge, entrance into the best life has to offer by being "in the know."

More than that, the academic disciple begins to exude the self-righteousness of the old Pharisee. Unless we know the right phrases, buzzwords, and "in" topics, unless we are "in the know," we are outsiders, despised and rejected by the intellectual snobs who believe God is summed up in their latest systems, concepts, and theories. Alas, many of our colleges and seminaries tend to be caught up in intellectual Phariseeism, a kind of irrelevant academic snobbery content in publishing books and papers largely to be read by their peers.

The academic types tend to be like those who say, "Lord, Lord," but never do anything Jesus asks them to do. They tend to be like those described by James who say to needy people, "Be warmed, be filled and clothed, and go your way," without ever giving them the food and clothing they need to be warm and full. As Paul once put it, "Knowledge puffs up, but love builds up." The Mother Teresas of the world know what he means.

The academic types emphasize being as opposed to doing. If they criticize the activists for acting without thinking, the activists criticize them for thinking without acting. If they invariably delay action by appointing study committees ad infinitum, activists tend to do *now* and to ask questions later. Academics want to serve God, but usually only in an advisory capacity. They tend to withhold commitment and involvement. And the answers to the burning religious questions are, observed Soren Kierkegaard, promised in their next book, which only raises more questions, with answers delayed to yet the next book.

Academic types tend to be disciples at second hand, whereas Jesus is looking for disciples at first hand, says philosopher Soren Kierkegaard — disciples who take the leap of faith, who make the commitment of both thinking *and* acting, of being *and* doing, of reflecting *and* recruiting.

The fanatic types lead with their hearts, the academic types with their heads. If like Peter, the fanatics want the Kingdom of God right now, the academic types like John tend to be mystical, reserved, and thinking of a Kingdom of God in some distant future. If the fanatics embarrass the academics by their energy and action, the academics embarrass the fanatics by their wisdom and foresight. If the fanatics tend to be self-righteous about how much they have done, the academics tend to be self-righteous about how well they have thought.

Neither fanaticism nor academism by themselves will do for discipleship. The word "disciple" means "learning follower." It is the root of the word "discipline." And the discipline required of Jesus' disciples is thinking *and* acting, learning *and* following.

You may be like me — not much of a fisherman. But Jesus calls all to renewed discipleship, to follow him toward new goals and priorities, to be faithful fishers of men, like Peter, Andrew, James, and John. And look how they changed the world.

Prayer

Eternal God, who has brought us to life in this world, wonderful and sometimes strange, and who has created us for worship of something higher than ourselves, we give you praise and thanks for your gifts to us.

You have not abandoned us in the universe, but through law-givers, prophets, and apostles, through poets, writers, and artists, through musicians, thinkers, and researchers, through ministers, counselors, and teachers, we have received the words of enlightenment and the spirit of inspiration. And now, in these latter times of your grand scheme of things entire, you have spoken to us through your son Jesus, who has become your very Word for us. How impoverished our lives would be without all the literature, music, art, architecture, and grace and love inspired by him. We give thanks for your revelation and guidance by means of Jesus.

It is for us to confess our waywardness and fickle devotion to what we have learned from Jesus. The pressures of daily life, the challenges to get ahead, the search for approval and approbation from our peers sometimes cause us to forget the loyalty and allegiance we once swore to Jesus as Lord and Master. We acknowledge we have paid more attention to our doubts than to his challenge to doubt our doubts. Determined to keep up on the daily news, we have neglected the eternal truths to be found in your Word. Striving to be "in the know" for the present age, we have avoided searching for the truths for the age to come. Forgive our dalliance and diffidence, O God, and empower us anew for more devoted discipleship.

We pray not only for ourselves, but also for all our brothers and sisters of the faith throughout the world. Especially do we ask you to bless with wisdom and strength the Christians of Eastern Europe and the former Soviet Union. Help them be faithful disciples to give new leadership toward a grand new life for their people. For the church in China we ask encouragement and faith and sagacity, that it might continue its faithful witness even in times of adversity. And for churches in this land, in this city, in this very place, we pray renewed vision and strength. Help us all once again to give up worship of the self or money or nation, to deny ourselves, to take up our crosses of discipleship to follow our Lord into the new age he has prepared for us. In Christ's name we pray. Amen.

A New Kind Of Teaching

Mark 1:21-28

Teachers and teaching have been with us since the world began. Early man taught his children how to survive — how to hunt, how to plant and harvest, how to provide shelter and protection, how to fight, how to raise his family in the tribal ways.

Learning and teaching took a great stride forward in classical Greece 450 years before Christ with the arrival of Socrates and his brilliant student, Plato. The radiant light of learning was passed on from Plato to Aristotle, and the world ever since has been their beneficiary.

Teaching and learning declined in the so-called Dark Ages and Medieval period, only to be revived by the Renaissance, the Reformation, and the Enlightenment. Public schools, colleges, and universities began to proliferate across the landscape of Western Civilization to cause the general educational level to rise like a giant tide lifting all of life to a higher plane.

Only a few short years ago education was an option in this country, but now it is law. And in this great nation we have more students in college or university than ever before anywhere in history. Learning is a way of life, teaching an honored and powerful profession.

But it is an increasingly difficult profession. Some believe a college is best defined as a log with an earnest student on one end and a brilliant, sympathetic teacher on another. Others scoff at such simplistic notions as they proudly point to their highly technical learning laboratories and complex information retrieval systems.

Not only is educational theory debated; educational practice is positively staggering. Think for a moment of the amount of information available. Our federal government, for example, generates over 100,000 reports each year, in addition to over 450,000 articles, books, and papers. Who on earth reads all that? Add to that the 60,000,000 pages a year of scientific and technical literature produced in the world plus the 365,000 books written each year, and you have an absolutely overwhelming amount of information. Furthermore, the information, the amount of knowledge, doubles every ten to fourteen years (cf. Alvin Toffler, *Future Shock*, p. 30 ff.).

Who on earth is going to sort all that out? How are they going to decide what to leave out? Who will teach it and how? Furthermore, what possible relevance does Jesus, a somewhat archaic Galilean teacher of over 1,900 years ago, have for us today amidst all our new information? Years ago his hearers were amazed at what he had to say and remarked that he taught them as one having authority, not as the scribes and Pharisees. They all recognized it as a new kind of teaching.

Even amidst the avalanche of information today, I believe his words still come across as a new kind of teaching, and Jesus as a new kind of teacher.

I

For one thing Jesus' teaching was new because it involved *commitment*, not just *comment*.

You probably remember the old definition of a lecture as the process wherein the information in the professor's notes is transferred to the student's notebooks without going through the minds of either!

That often is the case with teaching that is mere commentary. It assumes, like the old scribes and Pharisees, that truth is to be found only in the musty pages of the past. Consequently, teaching degenerates into a boring recitation of what someone else thought years ago, adding a little here, subtracting a little there.

Many teachers are mere technicians of information, rearranging facts and opinions in new ways, without ever taking a stand existentially, saying here is where I stand, here is where I stake my life. Colleges, universities, and graduate schools can become mere junctions of information and dispatchers of knowledge without ever being creative and existential, and thus authoritative.

When Martin Luther began publishing abroad his new teaching, the time came for him to take a stand and he took it. The gentle and scholarly Erasmus advocated many of the same ideas as Luther, but he had not the courage to take his stand so boldly. Scholars sometimes quip, somewhat inaccurately, that Luther hatched the egg Erasmus laid. Nevertheless, when Luther was called before all the ecclesiastical and political power of medieval Europe to answer for his teachings, as to whether they were his, he replied: "I am bound by the Scriptures I have quoted and my conscience is captive to the Word of God. I cannot and I will not recant anything, for to go against conscience is neither right nor safe. God help me. Here I stand, I cannot do otherwise. Amen." No wonder Luther's teaching had a ring of authority heard all over the world. He staked his life on it.

Amidst the blizzard of information available today, you can be sure we are on to something significant when the teacher begins to stake his reputation, even his life, on it. Talk is one thing, but commitment to the subject matter of the talk is quite another.

As in Luther, so in Jesus we have a man who takes a stand on what he is saying. Many of the scribes and Pharisees of Jesus' time taught dogmatically, which is to say, out of a rigid past and unimaginative present. Consequently, even though they taught dogmatically, they did not teach authoritatively, because they were not themselves existentially involved. They did not really enter into the situation. They gave textbook, stale answers. The hard, agonizing questions of life were referred to superficial solutions of the past, the pat approaches of a dry faith.

Not so with Jesus. He took the risk, entered into the situation, moved beyond the outdated rigidities, and spoke to the present need with clarity, insight, and conviction. When he spoke, you knew he was sincere, and not just mouthing the party line. You had the feeling that, if necessary, he would stake his life on what he was saying. He was not just a spectator-commentator observing the news.

He was committed to making the news. His was a new kind of teaching.

II

Note further, Jesus' teaching had authority because he regarded his hearers with *concern*, not with *contempt*.

Once in a while when I am out of the city someone will suggest I record my sermon in advance to be played on Sunday. Imagine that! I never do, because I always am reminded of a cartoon I once saw. The first panel of the cartoon showed a professor lecturing to a full classroom. The next picture shows a full classroom of students, but no professor. In his place was a tape recorder, giving his words of wisdom for the day. In the next picture, the professor's recorder is again giving out his lecture, but this time in place of a roomful of students, we have a roomful of students' tape recorders impersonally recording the impersonal lecture!

College and university students of today have suffered considerably from lack of exposure to top-notch teachers who personally care about them. Frequently students will enroll in certain institutions to study under their renowned authorities, only to discover they rarely, if ever, see them. Usually they are left to the devices of an unknown graduate assistant, or they listen to the outstanding authority along with 600 others in the once-a-week lecture series. Frequently our best scholars are caught up in research and publishing, with little personal contact or apparent concern for their students.

Other scholars show contempt for their learners by being as obscure as possible. They teach in riddles and play games to make learning unnecessarily difficult. This very often exhibits the defensiveness and insecurity of the professor. He may be threatened by the brilliance of his students and thus cloaks his limited knowledge in pretentious sophistication.

Jesus never played those kind of games with people. Rather he manifested a deep concern for all who would learn from him. He used simple stories drawn from the experiences of daily life to illustrate his deepest truths. He exhibited far more concern for the message of the Kingdom than for his reputation. Far from withdrawing to an inner circle of intellectual elitism, he ventured out into the countryside and marketplaces and synagogues to make known his views. He loved people and wanted to help them, so he spoke as plainly as possible. No wonder, then, that "the common people heard him gladly."

Most all disciplines of learning have their own jargon. Technicians, doctors, economists, lawyers, theologians, and ministers have their in-group language. A man once told me he never could figure out what ministers were talking about until he studied a little philosophy. Admittedly, some sermons are like reading an insurance policy or legal contract. You never are quite sure what has been said. Perhaps we all withdraw into the security and protection of our businesses and professions because we are afraid and want to protect our corner on things by being obscure.

But Jesus' teaching had a ring of authority, a newness, because he was concerned about his hearers. He wanted them to understand, to know, to learn. So concerned was he that he risked himself, shared himself with his audience. No phony manipulation on his part. No false, gimmicky tricks to get his people to open up while he remained closed. Rather, with him we find a genuine openness, an inner confidence. When we listen to him, we encounter an authentic person, not a shifty, money-grubbing writer of pseudo-books. No wonder his was a new kind of teaching. It was the authority of his whole loving person behind it.

As New Testament scholar B. Harvie Branscomb puts it: "Herein was Jesus' contribution — himself. By virtue of the fact that he embodied his ideal, what he said was living and vital and impelling. For religion is a personal thing. It can never become an abstract principle. It is a way of life" (*The Teachings of Jesus*, p. 368). Seeing his hearers as sheep without a shepherd, he gave himself to them. He communicated personally his love and compassion.

III

Once again Jesus taught with authority in his kind of teaching because he had a cure for the *demons, not just consolation.*

I realize it has not been popular to think of the reality of the demonic until recent years with movies like *Rosemary's Baby* and *The Exorcist* which drew record crowds. Jesus took the demonic seriously, as do some present-day psychoanalysts. Rollo May says, "The demonic is any natural function which has the power to take over the whole person. Sex and eros, anger and rage, and the craving for power are examples." Today we sometimes would call demon possession by the word "psychosis." "The demonic," says Dr. May, "becomes evil when it usurps the total self without regard to the integration of that self" (*Love and Will,* p. 123).

The demoniac Jesus encountered in the Nazareth synagogue was possessed perhaps by a number of demons — demons of hate, guilt, rejection, passion, revenge. As often is the case with demoniacs, the sensibilities and perceptions are greatly heightened, almost to the point of a divine madness. Consequently, upon seeing Jesus, he shrieked, "What do you want with us, Jesus of Nazareth? Have you come to destroy us? I know who you are — the Holy One of God" (Mark 1:24). Deeply conscious of the inner workings of the psyche, Jesus named the demon, establishing power over him, and ordered him out of the man. Thus the man was at peace.

Some will remember William Golding's book, *Lord of the Flies.* A number of small boys are the sole survivors of a shipwreck on a remote island. In their effort to survive, they soon develop a society, rather primitive in form. Evil soon becomes an experienced reality. An old decaying pig's head, surrounded with worms and flies, becomes for them a deity, a god, a "Lord of the Flies," which being re-translated means "Beelzebub," the "Prince of Darkness and Decay."

In their fear and perverted imagination, the stranded boys began to believe the Lord of the Flies was demanding a sacrifice — a sacrifice of one of the boys whom they regarded as a troublemaker, because he was not a believer in their god of the underworld. The boys projected their fears to Piggy, the plump, bespectacled boy who tried to keep a balanced head and common sense.

Thus in their fear and obsession, they start their hunt for Piggy to sacrifice him to their demon-god. The frightening chase finally leads out to the beach. Running for his life, and losing, Piggy runs abruptly into a strong, clean, well-built man. The rescue party had arrived, and the demons were halted. Order and love and sensibility had arrived just in time. By the authority of sanity and civilization, the demons were repelled, and Piggy was saved, as were the other boys.

Humankind, stranded on this space island, has done its share of sacrificing to demons — the demons of war, hate, revenge, perverted sex, unbridled lust for power, uncontrolled greed, distorted ambition. Like Piggy, many of us have been running desperately along the beaches of the world, hoping against hope for the arrival of a rescue party.

As Christians, we now can announce that that rescue party has arrived in the person of the strong man, Jesus. Balanced, integrated, imbued with power, he calls the demons by name, thwarts their power, casts them out, bringing peace out of our demonic frenzy. And to all who submit themselves to his teaching he casts out the demons, calling them by name — fear, guilt, envy, jealousy, lust, negativism, slander, deceit, revenge, greed. Uncontrolled, these demons will destroy life on this beautiful island in space.

Sociology, history, philosophy, and psychology have a certain kind of power, but not the power of Jesus. Other teachings have authority but not the authority of Jesus' new teaching. Other intellectual disciplines give us self-knowledge, but the more clearly we see ourselves, the more we realize our powerlessness to realize our true aspirations, says Swiss psychiatrist Paul Tournier. "Then it is no longer of healing alone that man stands in need, but of salvation; of the assurance that the world and he have been redeemed," says Tournier (*The Meaning of Persons,* p. 110-111). We believe Jesus brings that new kind of teaching, the authority of salvation, wholeness, health, and fulfillment.

A woman once came to me to talk about her son in college. He had been getting involved with a rather conservative Christian campus group, and she was worried, fearing the kind of Christianity they were teaching. I advised patience, believing more good than harm would result.

Sometime later we talked again. An unbelievable change had come over her son. Whereas once he had been, in her words, a little spoiled rich kid obsessed with his own selfish concerns, he now was generous, thoughtful, outgoing, and determined to help others.

What had happened? He had fallen under the spell of a new kind of teaching, the teaching of Christ. The demons of selfishness, contempt, and greed had been cast out by the authority of Christ. He was a new man, and now he is helping make a new world as a missionary.

It's a new kind of teaching — a teaching with commitment, not just comment; concern, not contempt; cure for your demons and mine, not just consolation.

Prayer

Almighty God, in whom light and truth dwell eternally, and in whom there is no darkness at all or shadow of turning, we who live in the twilight zone of knowledge come to you for clarity of mind and purpose. Sometimes we have congratulated ourselves for humankind's educational progress. We have pointed to our learned faculties, our hallowed campuses, our impressive libraries and laboratories.

Yet, what are all these but feeble glimpses into the light of thy truth, O God. Your foolishness is wiser than all the Phi Beta Kappa wisdom ever collected. The intelligence of our most gifted geniuses is but a candle in the sunlight of your blazing radiance.

Therefore, we come to you, Lord God, Eternal Mind of the universe, confessing the darkness of our minds, the limitations of our wisdom, the confusions of our ignorance. We acknowledge our readiness to become puffed up with what little we know, our quickness to believe that we have it all sorted out and in order, that we have a good grasp on reality.

O God, forgive our arrogance. Bring into our lives additional glimmers of the light of truth. Break the self-righteousness of our cranial arthritis. Loosen the stiffened joints of our minds and spirits, that we might be freed up to think your thoughts after you.

We pray especially for the thinking of our world leaders. Bless and strengthen all those politicians who place our country's interest above their own. Help them not to be weary in well-doing. O God, help our land, and bring us to good health again. Help us repent of our arrogance and trust again in you, that we would have a teachable spirit, O God.

We pray for wisdom to find new, safe energy sources. Bless our scientists and technicians. Grant them insight into new sources of power. Through Jesus Christ our Lord. Amen.

The Need For A
Community Of Healing

Mark 1:29-39

A friend of mine finally came home from the hospital. He came home alive. For many long weeks there was real fear he would not come home at all. A week or so prior to Thanksgiving he entered the hospital with an emergency illness. After a few days, however, it became apparent something far more serious was wrong. Doctors were baffled.

More specialists were called in who eventually diagnosed his malady — a serious one indeed. Appropriate drugs and medications were administered, but his condition worsened. New specialists were summoned, new tests were conducted, but soon another very serious problem developed. New drugs and treatments were introduced, and then a third, perhaps even more serious, problem evolved.

One day his exhausted and desperate wife said to me, "What have we done wrong to deserve all this? For what sin are we being punished?" Devout Christians, my friend's wife said they had been faithful in church, that they attempted sincerely to live the Christian life, and that they believed in God and Jesus Christ. "Why then," she asked, "is all this happening to us? It seems like a bad dream. I just can't believe it."

Sooner or later most of us are confronted with serious illness or disease or injury. And like my friends, many of us will wonder if we are being punished for some public misdeed or secret sin. Harboring as we do a reservoir of guilt deep within our breasts, some of us may feel the justice of God is being visited upon us.

The Gospels reflect a similar attitude. In the popular mind of Jesus' day it was assumed sickness was due to sin. Of the man born blind it was asked whether his or his parents' sin was the cause of his infirmity. Jesus regularly told those he healed to go their way and sin no more, implying their illness was associated with their sin. In the lesson from Mark, Jesus advises his critics and followers that healing and forgiveness of sins and casting out of demons somehow are connected.

But is that true today? Do we understand sin and sickness that way? But equally important, how do we go about achieving wholeness and health and healing? I believe the stories of Jesus' healing provide a model for a community of healing.

I

For one thing, notice that the friends of the sick cared about them. They not only brought them to the good physician without an appointment; they boldly gathered and waited outside the door. They had carried and assisted their sick friends and family members. Now they prayerfully awaited their cure.

Nevertheless, one thing is apparent — these people cared about their friends. They were doing everything in their power to cure them. Yes, they were bold and impetuous, perhaps even ludicrous. But this is clear — they loved their friends and they were convinced Jesus could help them.

My sick friend's wife said for a long time in the hospital they didn't seem to be making any progress. But one day, she sat the busy doctors down and said, "Look, we're not getting anywhere. My husband is getting worse and you have no answers. I believe the medical profession can help him. Call in any specialist from anywhere. Or if you think I should take him to the Mayo Clinic or New York or anywhere, I will take him. But he needs help, and I am determined to see that he gets it." Her family and friends also were determined, and, believe me, they got results. They put her husband into the middle of the best specialists available. Eventually healing began to take place.

One of the great fears we all have in a time of illness is that of being abandoned, neglected, and forgotten. While many of us may not feel we are being punished for some sin during our illness, we may, nevertheless, be ashamed of our weakness and our inability to cope. Confident, independent, and self-sufficient, many of us find it difficult to be in a position where we are weak, helpless, and vulnerable. We know our family and friends enjoy us in our strength, but we wonder if they will stand by us in our weakness. They often have enjoyed the pleasure we have brought them, but now we worry if they will love us when we bring them the burden of pain.

Like the sick of Jesus' day, and like my desperately sick friend, we all need a community of friends to surround us, to support us, and to bring us to the good physicians. We need to be assured we will not be rejected or abandoned or forgotten. We need someone to plead our case during our weakness, someone to hold up our cause. We need a group to be an offensive line against ineptness and inefficient medicine and the inertia of indifference. Our friends need us, and we need them. We need a community of healing. And we can be one.

II

Note further that the friends of the sick people not only cared enough to bring them to the good physician. They cared enough to pray in their behalf. They came to Jesus in faith, asking him to heal their friends.

I am convinced one reason my friend came home from the hospital is because his family and friends prayed for him. Medically speaking, my friend and some of his illnesses are still very much a mystery. Despite all the advanced technology and highly sophisticated techniques, they are not yet altogether sure what was wrong.

One day while visiting my friend, he said he felt he could make it if only he could get some kind of inner peace. Deep within his being something was wrong, he said. There was an imbalance, a distress, an anguish which prohibited an inward strength he felt necessary for healing. He read the book of Job, as did his wife, and said at one time he felt God was testing him. At other times in

113

his complete exhaustion he barely could talk and would only whisper a faint thank you when I would tell him our church was praying for him, as was, of course, his own church, and others. On stronger days he would thank us with great sincerity in both eyes and voice.

This went on for several weeks as he hovered between life and death. But then one day I saw it in his eyes. The peace had come, a corner had been turned, and slowly, but gradually, he was on his way to recovery. What made the difference? Good medicine and expert specialists to be sure. But he and his wife also will tell you that the prayers made the difference. In the near total exhaustion and bleakest moments, they claim they were sustained by faith and prayer — their own, and the faith and prayer of others when they were too weak to pray for themselves.

I have had many people tell me that. One man told me that when his minister took his hand to pray for him in the hospital, he could feel the healing power of love flow from the minister to himself. Soon he was home. Another told me as she lay in the hospital bed she just opened herself to receive the healing power of prayers being said in her behalf. It was as though she were being flooded with the color of deep purple. She experienced great peace and inner strength. Another lady told me she didn't know what Christian friends meant until she entered the hospital and they surrounded her with concern and prayer. These and many others I have known have been healed because friends have brought them to the good physicians and have prayed to the Physician of us all. The Church can and should be that kind of healing community. In a lonely world of hostility and alienation we need that kind of concern.

III

Note further that in the story of Jesus and the sick, healing and the forgiveness of sins are associated.

It may be that some illnesses are caused by sin. I know that many psychosomatic diseases are caused by fear and guilt and anxiety. A lady in another city had been seriously ill with arthritis for years and was taking at least sixteen special tablets or capsules a day. Though married for 31 years the relationship with her husband had not been good for a long time. However, despite her pleading, the husband refused to go for counseling or to talk with her about the marriage. Consequently, she sued for divorce. Strangely, she now has no sign of the arthritis which pained her for years.

However, let us not misunderstand. We are not saying that all people with arthritis have unhappy marriages. I know people with arthritis who have happy marriages. Nor are we saying that divorce was the best solution in this situation. We only are saying that it was one solution that made a dramatic change in the health of the wife. Further, we are not saying that all disease is psychosomatic. We only are saying that some diseases have psychological origins. Consequently, when the psychological distress is relieved, the physical problems fade away. Or to say it theologically, when the sins are forgiven, the bodily ailment is cured.

Doctors know that a large percentage of their patients have problems of the soul more than problems of the body. Disorders of the nervous system such as heart disease and ulcers may have origins in the soul which is "ill at ease." There is even the hint that some forms of cancer may be linked to psychological distress. Note that we are *not* saying all diseases have psychological origins. We only are saying that some, perhaps many, do, and that healing in such instances will have to deal with the psyche and the soul, as well as the body.

Consequently, when Jesus healed people he often directed his efforts toward the mind and soul of the patient. When he saw the sick, he may have seen people constricted with fear. Perhaps he saw people frozen under the spell of guilt or immobilized by anxiety. But because of the faith of the friends, and because of the excitement and expectation of the crowd, and because of the penetrating power of Jesus' presence, the sick were assured of release from the guilt that enslaved them. And they became whole.

For the majority of us, I suppose fear and guilt do not cause bodily paralysis. Our malady more commonly is a paralysis of spirit, a bondage of the will. We may well continue to move our arms and legs; our difficulty is getting something going in our frozen personal relationships. Many of us have no special problem

115

with physical mobility. Our hang-up is impotence in social, economic, and political spheres.

A community of healing can help us by stimulating us out of our paralysis of will. If others expect a certain level of performance from us, we often are motivated to live up to their expectations. If surrounding us we have those who care about us, who want to see us develop, who wish to build us up rather than tear us down, we have a good chance of becoming whole. If we are supported by a believing, loving, encouraging group, our chances for healthy survival are greatly enhanced. And a church can be a caring, loving, helping support group, rather than a bickering, manipulative, competitive, volatile, highly politicized, stress-causing group. Despite all our claims of independence and self-sufficiency, we really need one another. In mutual love and concern we can bind up the wounds and release our souls from disease.

My friend is home from the hospital and is on the road to recovery. I do not know why some people are healed and others are not. But I do know this: when people are surrounded by good doctors and a caring, praying community, healing very often occurs. And, even if persons die, they do so knowing that they have not been rejected or abandoned or forgotten, but that they have been loved. And for many, that is enough; for love lasts forever, because God is love.

Prayer

Eternal God, whose power calls a universe into being, and whose presence sustains life and breath upon the face of the earth, we are drawn to you by awe and imaginings beyond our control. In dreams and visions and many splendored things you speak to us of mysteries and marvels which draw us out of ourselves into larger realms of reality. In the bread broken and the cup of water given, you challenge our selfishness and remind us of love's gentle power, its fragrant renewal.

In the word of forgiveness spoken and the aid of a patient, gentle man, you lure us into lifestyles of giving rather than taking, blessing rather than seeking to be blessed. We thank you, Lord, for this upward call to a nobler humanity.

We come to you, our God, out of the anguish of a broken world — of broken bodies and hearts and souls. Even now our hospitals minister to those in pain, those whom disease and accident and quirks of nature overcame. We do not understand why so many should be ill, but we do know it is your design that we be whole and well and therefore holy. Grant, we pray, the blessing of healing and wholeness to those close to us.

We pray for all ministers and agents of healing, especially those of this community. We ask your wisdom and grace for our hospitals, that they might be places of joy and wholeness. We pray for all nursing homes and nurses, for all doctors and residents and interns. We ask your guidance for all scientists and researchers, that new discoveries might be made to enhance healing. Bless our medical schools, that they might be devoted unselfishly to training for the task of healing. For our special problems in medicine, we ask your guidance, O God; for the malpractice issue, for high costs, for matters of national health insurance, for genetic research and abortion, for euthanasia and transplant issues, we ask your wisdom, O God.

We pray also for those who need healing of mind and heart and soul. Let your grace work through psychiatrists, psychologists, counselors, and ministers. Let us experience again your power of healing and wholeness in the deep reaches of our being, that in this fragmented age our lives may know the beauty of your peace. Through Jesus Christ our Lord. Amen.

Love, Medicine, And Miracles

Mark 1:40-45

It was the cover story in *Psychology Today*. In another time it might surprise us, but in this age of change and discovery and searching for new, adequate meanings for life and health, it may not seem as unusual. The bold cover headlines state, "Spiritual Healing Hits The Suburbs."

Excerpted from a newly released book, *Ritual Healing In Suburban America* by Meredith McGuire and assistants, the article focuses on unconventional ways of understanding our illnesses and unconventional ways of treating them. If spiritual diagnosis and spiritual healing were earlier assigned by sociologists to the lower classes and primitive peoples, it is now the middle and upper middle classes who have been searching out a deeper meaning to illness and finding cures outside the traditional biological understanding of medicine.

The author found that these alternative understandings and practices were not something to which people resorted when all else failed. Instead, "most adherents we found were initially attracted by that larger belief system which provides, among other things, an alternative explanation of the origins of illness and a specific theory of health, deviance and healing power" (*Psychology Today*, Jan.-Feb. 1989, p. 58).

In contrast to popular notions about such groups, little money changes hands. Instead, most spiritual healing groups tend to be religiously or psychologically based, where love, mutual support, and caring encouragement are shared. Most all groups call upon a higher power for healing, whether that power is called God, Divine Mind, cosmic energy, or inner resources within the person.

Typical medical personnel, says the author, tend to ignore the more personal aspects of illness to treat the patient as a "case." But the new groups "spiritualize rather than medicalize" issues relating to health. "They challenge the medical model of healing by redefining the sources of illness and individual responsibility for (them)" (*ibid.*, p. 59).

The authors would be in agreement with a spate of books in recent years speaking of alternative ways of diagnosing illness and effecting treatment and cure. One of the most popular of such books is Dr. Bernard Siegel's *Love, Medicine and Miracles*, which was on *The New York Times* best-seller list for many weeks. A practicing surgeon and professor at Yale University, Dr. Siegel speaks movingly of his own conversion to a new way of seeing and of practicing medicine. In short, through faith, hope, and unconditional love, he has witnessed miracle after miracle. Accepting the findings that the majority of our illnesses are psychosomatic, he therefore proposes treatment which is psychosomatic in nature — treating both body and soul.

At first glance it would seem those of us in the religious community would be saying, "Of course, we've believed that all along. Look how much time and energy Jesus devoted to healing." But on second glance, it must be said that those of us in the religious community have become quite skeptical about spiritual healing. We have rightly suspected some of the faith healers to be perpetrating a hoax on naive, desperate, and gullible people.

We Protestants, smitten with a heavy dose of rationalism, have been suspicious of claimed miraculous healings at Roman Catholic religious shrines like Lourdes. Further, we Protestants of the Reformed tradition have often said miracles ceased with Jesus and the apostles. Consequently, we have even been negligent in praying for the sick, believing only in so-called "rational" cures.

But Dr. Siegel and others are calling us to shed our old ideas and narrowness of thought, to look at the larger realities which are breaking in upon us. The age of miracles is not over, especially for those with eyes to see. There are marvelous examples of miraculous healing taking place every day, says Dr. Siegel.

In that context, let us look again at the well-known story of Jesus' healing of the leper. Who were the actors in this story and what were the factors needed for healing? They may be remarkably similar to those suggested by Dr. Siegel.

I

Consider first the *leper*, the man who was healed.

In the time of Jesus, leprosy was a term applied to a variety of diseases which manifested themselves on the skin. Some of those diseases may well have had psychosomatic sources; that is sources which arise out of the *psyche*, or soul or mind, which in turn affect the *soma*, the body. Thus the leper might have had a psychosomatic or mind-body illness.

In his unique medical practice, Dr. Siegel has come to believe that a great many of our diseases are psychosomatic in nature. Dr. Bernard Fox of Boston suggests, for example, that depressed men are twice as likely to get cancer as non-depressed men. People full of hate and resentment are more susceptible to illness. Persons with low self-esteem are likelier to be ill than those with high self-esteem. Dr. Granger Westberg of the Holistic Health Care Centers believes fifty to 75 percent of illnesses originate in problems of the spirit rather than in brokenness of the body. And most any physician today would say that many of his or her patients have psychosomatic symptoms and illnesses.

We are not told how the leper in our story became ill. It could be the result of psychosomatic conditions. Some people have become ill as a result of a deep guilt complex. Others have become ill because of obsessive fear and insecurity.

Whether "leprosy" or illness, many of us have come to associate sickness with rewards, says Dr. Siegel. "We get to stay in bed and relax. People send us cards and flowers. Friends write and tell us they love us. Parents and spouses bring us chicken soup and read to us" (Siegel, *op. cit.*, p. 110). Sickness gives us the "permission" to do things we otherwise would be prohibited from doing.

We can say no to unwelcome burdens and duties and push them off on to others.

When the aged mother of a surgeon friend of mine died, I called on the family to spend time with them and to plan for the funeral. The mother had been in and out of hospitals and in and out of sickbeds many times. When we called on her before her death, she would recite, with some apparent pleasure, the long list of ailments and maladies she had endured.

Remembering that trait about his mother, my surgeon friend observed with lighthearted candor, "Yes, my mother has enjoyed ill health for many years!" He meant, of course, that through her illnesses, feigned or real, she could manipulate him and all the family to do her bidding. If the truth be known, she preferred not to be well. She wanted others to take the responsibility for her.

Another woman of my acquaintance was, in her younger years, a serious hypochondriac. As it turned out, her many illnesses, real or imagined, were a way of gaining the attention and services of her mother, who tended to ignore her and who tended to deny any kind of illness. It was a vicious cycle.

It may be the leper in our story was ill due to fear or guilt or hypochondria. He may have, as the saying goes, enjoyed ill health for years, with people pitying him and waiting on him hand and foot.

Whatever the past may have been, he is changing now. He is coming to see Jesus, the famous spiritual healer. He is tired of the past with all its hindrances, restrictions, and limitations. He now wants to be made whole. He wants to be well. He says to Jesus, "If you will, you can make me clean."

The leper, by coming to Jesus, has taken charge of his life, which is essential to healing, says Dr. Siegel. That puts him in the top fifteen to twenty percent, says the Yale surgeon. At the other end of the scale, about fifteen to twenty percent of his patients consciously or unconsciously want to die, says Siegel. The other sixty to seventy percent are in the middle, more or less playing the role the doctor assigns to them. But now, whatever his past, the leper is ready to be healed. He is ready to take responsibility for his illness and his cure. And he is ready for a miracle.

II

If the paralytic patient was a principal actor in this miracle story, so were the *friends* who believed him, accepted him, included him, and spread the good news so that "Jesus could no longer openly enter a town, but was out in the country; and the people came to him from every quarter" (Mark 1:45).

Whatever our illness, we need friends who support us, help us, and then who accept us and include us as healed persons, as well and as whole. We need people who want us to be well as much as we want to be well. We need a support group and agents of healing who believe we can be made whole.

Many of the agents for healing are found in hospitals. A father and his son, farmers from the boondocks, were making their first visit to the big city hospital. Standing in the hospital lobby, they saw an elevator for the first time. They watched an old cleaning lady, laden with bucket and mop, her body stooped and worn, revealing the ravages of labor and poverty, enter the elevator.

They watched the silver doors close and the numbers above the elevator light up, stop, then start down again. The silver doors opened and out stepped the most beautiful woman they had ever seen. The father turned to his son and said, "Quick, son, go get your mother!" Miraculous elevators or not, most of us need a support group. Dr. Siegel formed a support group known as ECP, Exceptional Cancer Patients. Here, cancer patients, as well as family and friends, listened to, encouraged, shared with, prayed for, and sustained one another to aid in the healing process.

As many of us know, illness can be relational, that is, it has to do with our relationships. A support group often can be a therapy group to help us be cleansed of hostility, resentment, anger, guilt, grudges, bitterness, and hopelessness. Very often, once the relationship has been made psychologically whole, the patient becomes physically whole.

III

But, of course, it was *Jesus* who was the main actor in this healing miracle. Jesus was the special agent of the divine power present in all healing.

The study of spiritual healing in the suburbs reported by *Psychology Today* notes that most all healing involves some contact with power outside oneself. To be sure, most all groups emphasize the power of the mind to effect bodily cure and the immense resources of spiritual power within each of us to aid in healing. Nevertheless, in addition to these and in addition to traditional medicine, there is emphasis upon God or universal mind or cosmic power. By participating in this divine source outside the self, healing is effected.

In our story, Jesus is the focus for eliciting the divine power and being put in touch with it. By his reputation and his powerful sense of presence, he was able to elicit faith from the leper as well as from his friends. Faith is essential for healing, says Dr. Siegel, faith in oneself, faith in one's doctor, faith in one's treatment, and faith in God or a cosmic, spiritual force. Jesus, like the good physician he was, had the power to elicit faith.

But even more, Jesus had the power to elicit love — the leper's love of God and love of himself. By healing the leper, Jesus in effect said that his sins were forgiven. Thus the leper could be released to love himself, to shed all the negative self-images which had been thrust upon him by family and friends, and to develop a healthy self-esteem.

Says Dr. Siegel, "The fundamental problem most patients face is an inability to love themselves, having been unloved by others during some crucial part of their lives" (*op. cit.*, p. 4). Thus, when Jesus pronounces forgiveness he says, "You are not the unloved, unwanted child any more. You are not the family scapegoat or the abused wife. The flaw within you which made you feel unlovable is now eradicated."

When Jesus says, "I forgive you," it is another way of saying, "I love you." When we forgive, it is our way of saying, "I love you." Your life is of infinite worth and is really no more flawed than anyone else's. Take charge of your life and walk into a healthy, whole life with your head up high, knowing you can love yourself because you are loved by the Son of God. And such affirmation, such love, says Yale's Dr. Siegel, is the most powerful stimulant of the body's immune system to ward off and defeat disease.

Following in the train of great spiritual healers like Jesus, Dr. Siegel emphasizes the importance of unconditional love in healing. Spirituality as exhibited in faith, forgiveness, peace, and love is always present in those who achieve unexpected healing from serious illness, says Dr. Siegel. Consequently, it is important for the patient to be full of hope and determination, to visualize himself or herself with new self-images where forgiveness has erased the past and has made possible the beginning of a new self and new relationships.

Follow good habits of nutrition, says the doctor. Exercise regularly, laugh a lot, refrain from smoking, drink only moderately, think positively rather than negatively, forgive, and you will be forgiven. Choose to be healthy and have the courage to heed the words of Jesus: "Your sins are forgiven. Be made clean."

And then it will be said as in Palestine long ago, "We have seen strange things here today."

Prayer

Eternal God, who loves the world with a steadfast love, and yet who keeps your distance from the world to give it freedom for development and growth, we praise you for the risks you have taken in bringing forth the world out of your own Being, to take a chance on love and freedom. Like a parent bringing forth children into the world, uncertain what the future holds, so you have brought us into being, unwilling to predetermine our every thought and move and action. We thank you for the gift of freedom which makes faith and hope and love more real.

In your presence, as students before the master teacher, it is for us to confess our frequent misuse of freedom. Some of us have been ignorant or smug, ignoring wise counsel or the wisdom of the ages. Some of us, out of fear and defensiveness, have rationalized our bad habits and justified our oppressive thinking. Some of us, refusing to mature spiritually and emotionally, remain infantile and dependent in our actions. Others of us, conceited and arrogant from the spoils of recent success, have changed liberty to license, forgetting our balanced relationship with you and one another. Forgive our frequent misuse of freedom, we pray.

If it is true we bring some of our illness and suffering upon ourselves because of misused freedom, it is also true disease and suffering come to us, from where we do not know. Look then with mercy and pity on all the weak and diseased, the sick and suffering peoples of the world. Come into each hospital and nursing home, each emergency room and refugee camp, each leper colony and psychiatric ward, each children's and veteran's hospital and sickroom at home, each cancer ward and surgical suite, and let your compassionate healing presence be made known with new force and power.

Almighty God, Divine Mind of the universe, let the power and influence of your positive thinking flow through us all with new force. If as lethargic or dull or conceited students we have been unwilling to think your new thoughts, help us to be open to you, to let your power and thinking flow through us to make us whole and well. If we have been overburdened with guilt or spiritually congested with resentment and hostility, cleanse our souls, that we might be unburdened and refreshed.

Oh how earnestly we pray for the sick and suffering. We pray for doctors and nurses, for technicians and administrators, for researchers and drug companies, for counselors, ministers, and psychiatrists, that new waves of your healing power might flow through them. Let this be an age of new wholeness and health, so that like you, we might be whole, and therefore holy. In Christ's name we pray. Amen.

Standing Room Only
Religion And Roof Repair

Mark 2:1-12

I long have enjoyed this story of Jesus' healing of the paralytic. It is a picturesque story containing drama, suspense, and humor. I have imagined the crowds pressing in upon Jesus in an effort to hear clearly the profound wisdom and good news he was sharing. There was an excitement in the air which goes along with being in the presence of a celebrity.

I also have imagined the delightful scene of the four friends carrying the paralyzed man, trying to press through the crowd into the packed house where Jesus was "preaching the word," as Mark puts it.

Frustrated in their efforts, they hit upon an idea. If they could not get *through* the crowd, they would go *over* the crowd. One can almost see the ideas click on in their minds as they focus on the outside stairway leading up to the flat roof of the house. And then I wonder about practical questions, like how four men could carry a paralyzed man on a stretcher up those stairs without dropping him.

If the man had not been paralyzed up to that point, he might now be paralyzed by fear! No doubt he was feeling like a lot of older or handicapped people who often are taken where they do not want to go, and are not taken where they want to go, when they want to go!

But these four men were persistent. They were determined their friend was going to see Jesus, the man of God who had a reputation for healing the sick. No doubt their strongest motives were altruistic. They genuinely wanted him to be well. But they

127

may also have had some less altruistic motives. Who knows how long they had been carrying their paralyzed friend?

If they went to a party, he had to be carried. If they went to a feast, he had to be carried. If they went to a meeting, he had to be carried. It would be a relief to everyone to have him healed, for, as we know, ill health can be a terrible burden to everyone involved.

Now on top of the roof, imagine the scene. Down below in the packed house, Jesus heard the clamor and thumping on the roof. Next there was the pounding and ripping as the four men began to tear up the roof made of branches and hardened mud. Down below, the dust and debris fell on Jesus and the crowd. And soon, being lowered right in front of Jesus was the paralytic on a stretcher, being lowered, perhaps by ropes, to the feet of Jesus. Talk about persistence and sparing no effort to get Jesus' attention!

I was reading this passage again a few weeks ago at home when I saw something I hadn't seen before. I said to my wife, "Look at this. Guess whose house they were in when all this took place? Whose roof was it that was torn apart by these exuberant, determined friends? Look, it says Jesus had returned to his own home in Capernaum on the shores of Lake Galilee." It was Jesus' roof these fellows were ripping up without permission. (Or possibly Peter's, as some scholars contend.)

While Jesus was preaching the Gospel to a standing room only crowd, his roof was being torn apart for the sake of the paralytic. Standing room only religion can lead to roof repair. But it can lead to a whole lot more. And that's what this wonderful story is all about.

I

There was standing room only religion because *faith was being expressed.*

Faith was being expressed in those four men who brought their paralyzed friend to Jesus. I long have marveled at the almost buoyant faith expressed by those four fellows. When you think of it, they could have hung back in laziness or cynicism or disbelief. They could have scoffed at all the weak women and children running after yet another deluded religious teacher. They could have

128

rested content in their skepticism and their conviction that there is, after all, nothing new under the sun, that as things have been, they always shall be.

They could have done that but they didn't. Instead, they put aside any latent fear or cynicism and carried their friend to Jesus in the hope and faith that something new could take place, that paralysis did not have to be the final condition of this man, that he could be liberated from this terrible infirmity.

And there is reason to believe the paralyzed man also had faith. The Gospel speaks of Jesus seeing their faith, meaning possibly the faith of the paralytic as well as the faith of the four friends. It was their faith that was an important ingredient in the healing that took place. They had heard of Jesus' healings throughout Galilee and they came to him with the desire and the expectation he could heal the paralytic.

Contrast this scene with Jesus' visit to his hometown, Nazareth. Recall how when he preached to them in the synagogue they were first amazed and then offended. Then, scoffing, they challenged him to do some of his signs and wonders and healings in Nazareth that he had done elsewhere. But the Gospel says that Jesus could do only a few mighty works there because of their disbelief. The Gospel then adds that he marveled at their disbelief.

It was true then; it is true now — if we are to be healed we have to *want* to be healed, and we have to have faith so we *can* be healed. I can hear someone say, "How can you say that? Doesn't everyone want to be healed?" And we reply, "Not always."

Not everyone wants to be healed. In his best-selling book, *Love, Medicine and Miracles*, Yale University's Dr. Bernie Siegel says that "about fifteen to twenty percent of all patients unconsciously, or even consciously, wish to die. On some level they welcome cancer or another serious illness as a way to escape their problems through death or disease" (p. 23).

Look again at our story, at the four friends. If the paralytic had thoughts about death, or if he doubted he could be healed, the faith of his friends literally carried him along. And that's what we often need when we are ill, the faith of friends to carry us along when our own faith is weak or faltering.

129

I remember when growing up in Wisconsin, the churches of our association had a group known as the Rope Holders Association. They got their name from this story where they imagined letting the paralytic down into the presence of Jesus by ropes. It was their faith and action, their rope-holding, that enabled the miracle to take place. The Rope Holders of Wisconsin raised money to help weak churches or to start new ones, to bring them to health and growth. Churches, like people, need "rope-holders," people of faith who believe we can be well and whole and are willing to take the risks to make it happen.

When we are sick, we do often feel alone and abandoned. Many people do not want to be around those who are sick, especially if it is a prolonged illness. We lose patience. We want to get on with our own life. Or we have enough problems of our own. And consciously or unconsciously we communicate our lack of caring to the sick.

But when we pray for them, when we surround them with prayer, praying each day for them, when we say, "You matter to us, hang in there," what a difference that can make in an indifferent world where so few people seem to care. When churches decide to stand up against illness and disease and to encourage people in faith and prayer, what a difference it makes. If we keep our faith and expectancy and love high, we too might have to suffer the problems of standing room only religion and roof repair.

II

There was standing room only religion because *forgiveness was being experienced.*

In Jesus' time it was widely believed that there was a direct connection between illness and sin. Recall, for example, the question that was put to Jesus about the man born blind. Was he born blind because of his sin or his parents' sin? Jesus replied that it was neither. On other occasions, such as the one in our text, Jesus seems to imply some agreement with the then current thinking that somehow sin and illness are interconnected.

However, before we proceed with that concept, we need to place before us a word of caution. Not all illness appears to be connected with the sin of the patient or even of the parents. For example, my nephew and his wife recently lost their baby girl who was born with a serious genetic defect. We can hardly say the baby girl was responsible for the defect. Nor can we blame the parents who are but carriers of genes, not creators of genes. As we know, there are certain congenital defects carried in the genes which seem to have no relation to the conduct of the parents.

It should also be observed that animals get sick. We once had a little, black, curly-haired dog, who, once in a while, would get sick. So we would take him, not to the confessional, but to the veterinarian for a shot, which he sensed was coming and which he didn't like.

While he was basically a very good and playful and intelligent dog, and while he regularly thought of himself as a "people" and as a full member of the family, he could, if the truth be known, misbehave from time to time. Like the time he left a dropping on my sermon manuscript!

Even though it took me some time to forgive him for that, I never really believed he knew what he was doing, even though some of my detractors in the church were convinced he did! Nevertheless, I never felt our dog should confess his sins, although I did have other thoughts about the detractors! Was there a connection between his illness and his misbehaving? I think not. Some diseases seem implicit in the stream of life.

That said, we need to look again at the psychological component present in many illnesses, says Dr. Siegel. And we need to realize our participation and responsibility in the disease process, says the Yale surgeon. This is not, he says, the same as blame or guilt. Rather, it is taking stock of our psychological and mental attitude with respect to our health.

Look again at our text. When Jesus saw the faith of the paralytic and the four friends he did not say, "Be healed." Instead he said, "My son, your sins are forgiven." In other words, Jesus may have seen in the man something that was the cause of the paralysis — some psychological problem perhaps, some guilt, some deep, unresolved conflict, some deep, unexplained fear which may have been implanted in his childhood.

In this highly charged situation of faith, he believed what Jesus announced, namely, that God takes no pleasure in the suffering and punishment of his people. Rather, it is his will that all people come to repentance to experience his grace and forgiveness, because the word "forgiveness" means to give the life back to start over again. Forgiveness means to release the grudges, to come back into the relationship to work for the common good. It means to let go the fears which too long have bound us.

Dr. Siegel stated whimsically that many of us develop our diseases for honorable reasons. Disease is the body's way of telling us that not all our needs are being met. And if we are suffering from depression we may be telling ourselves that our life is meaningless because our past can never be forgiven. Nonsense, says Jesus. Have faith. You are forgiven. Take up your sickbed and walk. You can be healthy and whole. Or as Harvard's William James put it, "The greatest discovery of my generation is that human beings, by changing their inner attitudes of their minds, can change the outer aspects of their lives" (Siegel, *op. cit.*, p. 111).

That's true in healing a marriage. One couple in another city could relate only by argument. Wherever they spoke they brought up the past and recited all the wrongs they had done to each other. In fact, they had a "Fibber McGee's closet" of grudges, and every time they opened the door of conversation all those saved-up grudges of the years came crashing out.

Until one day, after some counseling, they just decided to forgive each other. Yes, they had wronged each other. Yes, they had hurt each other. Yes, they had been angry at each other for not being perfect, for not living up to their projected expectations of what a perfect spouse should be.

But then it dawned on them that they were destroying no one but themselves. They had been anxious, dyspeptic, angry, hard, curt, and hostile and not infrequently sick. And no wonder. And then they learned to relax into the grace of God, like leaning back in a beautiful, bubbling hot tub, letting all the hostility and grudges go and then saying, "I give you your life back to start over again. Let's make all things new." And they did. And it was wonderful — a life of grace instead of grudges, and they were healed.

To be sure, there are many mysteries about diseases and their causes. There are many things we do not know. But this we do know — prayer and faith and forgiveness can make a difference in the healing process.

Standing room only religion? Can it happen again? It certainly can whenever genuine faith and forgiveness are expressed. Oh, by the way, when there are genuine faith and forgiveness, you never have to worry about roof repair. I have a hunch the healed paralytic was back the next day with his four friends fixing Jesus' roof.

Prayer

Eternal God, whose Mind is beyond our knowing, but whose Spirit penetrates to the farthest reaches of the universe and searches out the inmost secrets of our hearts, you know us better than we know ourselves. From you no secrets are hid, and in your presence all illusions and pretensions are done away to come face to face with yourself, reality itself.

We praise you, Holy Lord God, and in your holy temple, we make haste to confess our hardness of heart and pettiness of spirit. Presented with wonders beyond our imagining in the natural world, and recipients again and again of your gracious promise of forgiveness and life everlasting, we become nonchalant and blasé in the presence of such splendors. Be merciful to us, Almighty God, and with your infinite patience open again our eyes and ears that we might truly see and hear all the wonders you have in store for us.

And yet, O Lord God, for all the wonders and beauties and ecstasies of the world, there are also the ugliness, the wrenching pain, the heart-rending sorrow, the grip of guilt, the shattering grief, the dark nights of depression, the days of crudity, brutality, violence, and bloodshed. Oh, what a world you have made, O Lord, and we have made for ourselves.

So today we ask you to look into our secret hearts, to go past the facade to behold the loneliness, the inner anguish, the despair that will not loosen its grip, the sense of betrayal that will not let us

133

trust again, the battle with disease that threatens to do us in, the financial worries which make us wonder about the future, the troubles at our job which make us question whether we are in the right place.

Look then, O Holy and merciful God, our loving Father, upon the pain and brokenness of your children and grant us the strength and health, the healing and wholeness we need for the living of these days. Minister to each of us according to our several needs. Send out your light and heal and help us to look to you, that we might be radiant and buoyant in our believing.

Sometimes with the old spiritual we say: "Sometimes I feel discouraged, and think my work's in vain, but then the Holy Spirit revives my soul again."

Help us to believe: "There is a balm in Gilead to make the wounded whole. There is a balm in Gilead to heal the sin-sick soul."

Hear our prayers, through Christ our Lord. Amen.

Epiphany 8

Overcoming The Anxiety
Of An Inadequate Background

Mark 2:13-22

Americans are increasingly concerned about backgrounds. In the old days when immigration was fresh in our minds, we often were ashamed of our background and saw it as a hindrance to advancement in the new world. We wanted to throw off the old language, the old dress and cuisine, and the old culture, in our effort to be accepted in the new world.

Today, however, there is renewed interest in backgrounds. A sociologist has summarized the phenomenon in a "law" which says, "What the son wishes to forget, the grandson wishes to remember." The son, still concerned about old world vestiges in his personality and behavior patterns, and worried about total acceptance in the new world, in some ways envies the grandson, who feels totally accepted, totally Americanized, and delights in old world dances, language, clothing, cooking, stories, and customs.

Consequently, many Americans are turning to ethnic cooking, ethnic festivals, and ethnic languages. Others research their family tree and brag about their background until they find a skeleton in the ancestral closet! Someone even quipped lately that Alex Haley, author of *Roots*, discovered he was adopted!

Americans are also upward achievers. Thousands of people move from one economic class to another, one cultured educational group to another. Unlike England where class destinations seem to be inherited and frozen, Americans are upwardly mobile. Thankfully so, for this freedom of upward mobility, or for that matter downward mobility, may be one of the great factors of continuing democracy and creativity.

Nevertheless, as Americans ascend into new socioeconomic-educational classes, they become increasingly anxious about their inadequate backgrounds. It is sometimes with difficulty they confess that their father was a farmer, or an appliance repair man, or a factory worker, or a trucker, or a shoe salesman, or a carpenter, or a bus driver. And even if he was a lawyer or a doctor, there is always the question of whether he went to the right schools, or practiced with the right firm in the right city, or whether he was prestigious and successful.

There is an ironic twist in the American psyche today. Upward achievers, who naturally pride themselves on their accomplishments, seem now to want an adequate background to justify their achievements and to give assurance in the new social atmosphere.

In some places it is improper to ask about one's background. In Australia, for example, backgrounds are never brought up. That is because England used to exile all its rabblerousers, ne'er-do-wells, and criminals to Australia. Everyone was assumed to have a very inadequate background, and so no one inquired about what they already knew.

But not so in this country anymore. We are concerned about backgrounds because we feel so rootless, so lacking in continuing identity in this age of transition and rapid change. In an effort to know who we are, we seek an adequate background to establish our security and identity and to allay our anxiety.

In Jesus' time, those with "adequate" backgrounds were the Pharisees. Devout, disciplined, and thoroughly committed to their religious beliefs and practices, they were regarded as insiders, as people who had arrived, as persons who were "in" with society and especially "in" with God.

But Jesus was criticized for associating with tax collectors and sinners, with "outsiders," with those of an inadequate background. In answer, he said, "Those who are well," that is, those with adequate backgrounds, "need no physician, but those who are sick. I came," said Jesus, "not to call the righteous, but sinners; not to help the 'insiders' but the 'outsiders.' I came," said Jesus, "to help those who feel they have inadequate backgrounds."

I

For one thing, Christ helps us overcome the anxiety of not being accepted.

Young people are concerned about being accepted. Recently a student returned from college, informing her parents she desperately needed a pair of the latest "in" shoes. "But you would never be seen in those at your high school," said her mother. "Yes, but everyone wears them at college," said the daughter. "You're a 'nobody' if you don't wear these shoes."

If high school and college students are concerned about not being accepted, so are important Americans. President Nixon used to express anxiety over his not being included in the Eastern Establishment of breeding, education, money, and aristocracy. But commenting on Nixon's anxiety, Eliot Richardson, a former Attorney General, a typical representative of the Eastern Establishment, once said that when you are President of the United States, you are "in" and you decide who is "in."

Nixon had difficulty accepting his own acceptance by the American people. He was so anxious and insecure he went overboard with his Committee to Reelect the President, to make sure he would win by a landslide, and thus be more "in" than anyone in history. And yet soon he was "out."

Nixon's anxiety over his inadequate background also made it impossible to confess any wrongdoing. Upward achievers always are anxious to be accepted by the group just above them. In order to be accepted they must prove to themselves and to the group "above" them that they are worthy. This may include wearing the right clothes, going to the right plays or concerts, serving on the right community boards, behaving with a certain set of manners, referring to the right books or periodicals, making lots of money, or political success.

All that is common enough. But upward achievers cannot admit to any wrong, because the group above them might thereby exclude them. Upward achievers make no public confessions, because cynically they know those already included have done their share of wrong and just have not been caught; and idealistically, they think of themselves as just as good as the guy or gal above them.

Such was the case with Nixon. He and his defenders pointed out the shady dealings of previous presidents and politicians. Undoubtedly they were right. We are now learning as fact what long was rumored, that President Kennedy regularly was visited by prostitutes, in the White House, no less. There was no public outcry, no clamor from the press, no confession of wrongdoing. But Nixon was caught, the evidence did seem to support impeachment, and when support eroded in the Senate, he was forced to resign.

Instead of a cover-up, Nixon might have confessed and asked forgiveness. He might have relaxed into the grace of God, knowing he was included in something so much greater than our own country. In the house of God, he might have quieted the anxiety of his inadequate background, knowing God looks into the heart, not on external accoutrements. The power and prestige of men means little to an omnipotent God. Nations to him are a drop in the bucket, as dust on grocer's scales, says Isaiah. God seeks the man of humble heart, the woman of contrite spirit, the young person of genuine character. The release from the anxiety of an inadequate background could have been there for President Nixon.

Upward achievers are tempted to believe they can storm the kingdom of God the same way they storm the socioeconomic class above them. They are deluded by the idea that their anxiety is primarily sociological and economic, and that the cure for the anxiety is the next step on the rung. But experienced upward achievers know that is something like drinking salt water to quench your thirst. It only makes you thirstier.

The apostle Paul recognized that his anxiety was something deeper than social class, economic standing, or academic credentials. It was the anxiety of the self, the anxiety of identity, the anxiety of death and immortality. His was the anxiety of attaining life, of making a name for himself, i.e., of ensuring his immortality. Like the first Adam, he was anxious because he recognized he was outside Eden, outside Paradise, away from the tree of life. Thus, he attempted to achieve his way back to Eden, back to Paradise, to assure his immortality and allay his anxiety. But to no avail.

That is when he discovered the grace of God in Christ, i.e., God's acceptance and inclusion of those who have the humility to confess their ultimate anxiety, who have the wisdom to put aside all their anxiety-produced credentials for earned acceptance into Paradise, and to believe in God, to trust in him and his grace. After all, the cause of the ultimate anxiety was lack of faith and trust in God.

II
Christ also helps us to overcome the anxiety of having to succeed.

The goal toward which most upward achievers work is success. Success is the reward for diligent preparation, hard work, and clever maneuvering. Success, for upward achievers, symbolizes salvation. Salvation means wideness of life, wholeness of life. It comes from the same root as "salve," an ointment used for healing. Thus, salvation is the state of being healed, of good health and wholeness. It is the enjoyment of the fullness of life.

Many upward achievers think success is the key to salvation, or is in fact salvation itself. It rescues the self from anonymity and gives it freedom to ski in Aspen, to vacation in the Bahamas, or to tour the world in leisure or luxury. Others have a more modest view of success — a view that sees themselves as comfortably well off, with good health, a good name, and no financial worries.

Nevertheless, success, in whatever package, is seen as salvation. It gives one the fullness of life. Thus, in a nation of upward achievers, the most prevalent anxiety is that of success — the anxiety of getting it and keeping it. The anxiety becomes compulsive and obsessive if one attaches one's total identity to the goal of success. How can one be saved from an inadequate background? By achieving success, says our upwardly mobile population.

Paul says the grace of God releases us from the compulsion to succeed because we discover that we are acknowledged, recognized, and loved in spite of our inadequacies. In fact, when we confess our inadequacies, instead of trying to cover for them in the success syndrome, we discover a new kind of wholeness and contentment and release. The humble acknowledgment before God of our inability to achieve all we know we ought to achieve counts in effect as achievement for us, because it is the "achievement" of

139

faith, the achievement of a humble and contrite heart, so essential to salvation, to wholeness and healing, to the release from anxiety and the inward peace and connectedness God gives. To their great surprise, the "sinners" and "outsiders," those who had not achieved religious "success," were precisely the ones Jesus invited to his table.

The experience of God's grace calms the ultimate anxiety of upward achievers over their inadequate background. After all, if the Son of God says you have "arrived," you have "arrived."

III

Christ also helps us overcome the anxiety of mortality.

Philosopher Bertrand Russell once observed that every man wants to make himself god. And we might add every woman wants to make herself goddess. That is, we all want to ascend in self-importance to the place of omnipotence and immortality.

The ultimate anxiety is that of death. Will we be annihilated forever? Will we be forgotten in the dust of the universe? Is death the end of everything? And if so, what meaning does life have? Are we here for this brief flash of time for no purpose other than to produce, consume, procreate, and die?

Many people today believe that to be the case, that this is the only life, that there is nothing beyond. Consequently, they are resolved to make the good life the substitute for the heavenly life. In the New York area, a lush residential area developed around Lake Success and was regarded by some as entrance to the good life, as was residence in Westchester or shoreline Connecticut, or summer residence in the Hamptons of Long Island. In the Minneapolis area people settled in a place called Paradise Valley, and they thought it was. And in Grand Rapids, Michigan, there were people who lived around Paradise Lake. But I've been to all these places, and I'm not convinced they are Paradise!

Nevertheless, much of our obsession with the good life, the life of paradise on earth, arises out of our anxiety over death and mortality. If this life is all there is, we have to make the most of it. Pity those who are poor or who have cancer or arthritis or heart disease or insanity.

140

Connected with this anxiety is our obsession with hedonism — the love of sensuous pleasure. Hedonism is the bodily interpretation of life. Its goal is to achieve the ultimate bodily experience in comfort, sex, wine, food, travel, music, theater, and possessions. Pleasure is the freedom to feel what you want when you want. Thus the self acquires all the accoutrements essential to hedonism, to sensuous pleasure, to allay the anxiety of dying without ever having experienced the totality of life. In this context how strange Jesus' words: "Deny yourself, take up your cross and follow me." But of the hedonists Paul says, "Destruction is their fate, the belly is their god. They glory in their shame, those men of earthly mind" (Philippians 3:19 Moffatt).

"We, by contrast," says Paul, "are citizens of heaven, and from heaven we expect our deliverer to come, the Lord Jesus Christ. He will transfigure the body belonging to our humble state, and give it a form like that of his own resplendent body ..." (Philippians 3:20-21).

Therefore, we can be released from the ultimate anxiety of having to make a name for ourselves and of thus assuring ourselves we will be remembered in history. Some people believe the only immortality we have is what lives on in the memory of those who survive us. One of the saints of my church remarked that, knowing how short some people's memories were, he hoped his immortality rested on something more than that. It does, says Paul. Do not be anxious. God remembers.

And if in this body you have missed out on the ultimate bodily experience, or if you are handicapped, or if the life of one you loved was short, take heart, because God will transform this present body and give it a form resplendent and immortal like Christ's.

Know then that Christ has overcome the anxiety of an inadequate background, an inadequacy possessed by the whole human race since the fall of Adam. He has, by his grace and love and acceptance, overcome the anxiety of acceptance, the anxiety of having to succeed, the anxiety of immortality. "Those who are well have no need of a physician, but those who are sick," said Jesus. "I came not to call the righteous, the insiders, but sinners, the outsiders, those anxious about their inadequate background."

141

Prayer

Lord of the light of the new day, who blesses the world with the presence of your shining favor, and who upholds the world with your faithful word of power, we, your humble servants, praise you for your life and power.

As creatures of time and sense, we come to you to gain perspective on the world and ourselves. Caught up in the onrush of time's ever-flowing stream, we draw aside to you for reflection, for insight, and for help with life's most puzzling questions. Be pleased to grant us the help we most need.

In this season we pray for clarity of vision. Help us to see the truth about ourselves and to amend our ways. Expose our flaws of character, which we have covered with rationalizations. Deliver us from eyes filled with lust and greed, so that we might treat our neighbors as persons, not as things.

Release us from fixation on the present moment, the immediate circumstance, the pain or pleasure of the hour, to see beyond into your larger purposes for our lives. Help us remove the wooden beam in our own eye before we try to remove the splinter in our brother's eye.

Lord God, you have promised to give strength to the faint and exhausted, a new heart to those weary of the world. Grant us strength in this season to break out of schedules, habits, and routines which limit us and bring us down. Give us power to break out of old ways of thinking which embrace a narrow view of the past and which screen out the most impressive realities of present and future. Endow us with new strength to love in those places where we have entrenched ourselves behind walls of hate or indifference or revenge.

In a day when so much of our life is determined and regulated by institutions, we ask for their new birth. Enable the family to gain control of itself and to impart noble values and personalized ideas. Curb the excesses of government at all levels, that it may again see its purpose to serve people, not to harass them. Enlighten national leaders throughout the world, that exploitation and bloodshed might cease, and peace and prosperity for all ensue. For the institutions of law and medicine call to remembrance the basic need to do justice in the land and to heal and help.

Endow the Church here and throughout the world with a new birth of purpose and power, that her apathy and impotence might be replaced with energy and joy and the confidence of victory over evil. Through Jesus Christ our Lord. Amen.

Jesus And
The Competition

Mark 9:2-9

Perhaps no artist in history has expressed the tenderness and beauty, as well as the majesty and glory of the Biblical tradition, as has Italy's Michelangelo. Determined to become an artist against his father's wishes, he was apprenticed to Florentine artists at a young age. Legend has it that he got his beginning as a sculptor from a cast-off piece of marble ruined by other students. Under Michelangelo's hammer and chisel, the cast-off became a masterpiece.

Many Americans will remember seeing Michelangelo's famous *Pieta* at the New York World's Fair in Flushing Meadows in 1964-65. Brought here to be a part of the Roman Catholic exhibit, millions of people, including my wife and me, lined up reverently to observe this tender and beautiful masterpiece.

Sometime later, we had the privilege of visiting Italy. We went first to Florence and to the Academy of Fine Arts to see Michelangelo's famous sculpture of David, standing in giant glory, beneath the domed museum. And in the large corridor leading to David are four works of Michelangelo, dubbed *The Slaves.* The sculptures look incomplete because the human figures have only partially emerged from the stone; they are yet enslaved. I love the sculptures because I think they are great symbols of our true selfhood, struggling to be free from the stone rigidities which enslave us.

From Florence, it was on to fabled Rome, and, yes, of course, to magnificent St. Peter's and the Sistine Chapel. I will never forget the first time entering the hushed atmosphere of that fabled, sacred room and looking up to see Michelangelo's *Creation of Adam*, and then looking forward to the grandeur of the scene of the *Last Judgment*. Sculpting or painting or designing, Michelangelo was indeed an artistic genius. However, one of Michelangelo's sculptic masterpieces is off the beaten track. When last in Rome we made a point to see it. Arriving before the all-important Roman lunch hour had ended, we waited on the steps of the church for the doors to be unlocked.

When finally we entered the sanctuary, there it was — not as well lighted as it might have been — Michelangelo's magnificent statue of Moses. He was indeed bigger than life, muscular in the Michelangelo way, awesome, imposing with an assertive majesty. And then there was something else — something unusual, something which has both intrigued and amused viewers for centuries. This Moses has, of all things, horns. There they are, just above the ears, large horns on either side of his head. Think of it — a Moses with horns!

Strangely, this Moses with horns is related to our scripture texts. When Moses went up to Mount Sinai to speak with God, his countenance began to glow with a radiance and glory, hurtful to the eyes of mere humans. So when Moses came down from the mountain with the glory of the Lord radiating through him, he had to wear a veil so as not to blind the people. And in Michelangelo's sixteenth century Italy, that Hebrew word for "glory" or "radiance" was mistakenly translated "horns," and thus the Moses with horns.

In Mark's text we could, in Michelangelo's terms, have a Jesus with horns. For just as Moses went to the mountaintop to talk with God, so did Jesus, fourteen centuries later, go to the mountaintop to pray, to talk with God. And just as Moses' countenance became radiant with the glory of God, so did that of Jesus. Mark tells us that Jesus "was transfigured before them and his clothes became dazzling white" (9:2, 3).

The intention of the synoptic gospel writers — all three of them, Matthew, Mark, and Luke — is to show that we now have a new Moses. Just as Moses went up on Mount Sinai to receive the old covenant for his people, so now Jesus goes up on Mount Hermon to receive the new covenant for his people. As Moses was glorified by the presence of God, so is Jesus.

But in the vision, Moses and Elijah appear alongside Jesus, talking with him about his forthcoming death and exodus from death to life. When Peter proposed in his excitement and fear that they build three shrines to honor them, a cloud came over them, Moses and Elijah vanished from view, and they saw Jesus only and were advised to listen to him. In this vision it appears as though Jesus is beating out the competition.

I

Consider *first the competition of Moses.*

You will recall that in the transfiguration experience Moses appeared with Jesus and Jesus is talking with him. You will notice that Moses is not talking *to* Jesus, that is, lecturing him, nor is Jesus talking *to* Moses, that is, talking *down* to him. Instead, they are talking *with* one another, suggesting that the work of Jesus is a continuation of what Moses, the lawgiver, was doing.

Indeed, Matthew's gospel is quite purposeful in presenting Jesus as a new Moses. He divides his work into five parts, just as the Pentateuch, the works of Moses, is divided into five parts. Jesus is the new lawgiver and in Matthew he asserts that he did not come to destroy the law of Moses, but to fulfill it. Heaven and earth may pass away, but not God's law, says this new Moses. And he asserts the importance of exceeding the righteousness, that is, the law-keeping, of the scribes and Pharisees.

Nevertheless, in this transfiguration vision, when Peter suggests they build three shrines — one for Moses, one for Elijah, and one for Jesus — a cloud envelopes them. And then Moses and Elijah depart, they see Jesus only, and a voice from heaven reminiscent of Jesus' baptism says, "This is my beloved son. Listen to him."

How was Jesus doing among the competition? Very well, according to this revelatory experience of the disciples. Moses is withdrawn into the mists of the past and the glories of heaven, and Jesus, the new lawgiver, is here to supersede him.

147

Saul, later known as Paul, had a similar experience. An intelligent, energetic, and zealous devotee of Moses, Saul had a momentous conversion experience wherein he saw the Risen Christ, much like Peter, James, and John saw the Transfigured Christ. As a result of this life-altering experience, Paul became convinced that neither he nor anyone could keep the law of Moses perfectly so as to obtain salvation. Salvation, said Paul, comes through the free gift of grace obtained through Jesus' perfect obedience of God, and through his crucifixion and resurrection.

So Paul and his contemporaries went all over the Graeco-Roman world converting people by the thousands, then by the millions, to this Gospel, this good news that God accepts us by grace through faith. Salvation is not a reward for law perfectly kept, but a gift of grace grasped by the outstretched hand of faith. Salvation, said Paul, is not a matter of achievement, but of "receivement."

After three centuries of persecutions and martyrdoms, Christianity received new impetus from Constantine's vision and conversion. As Christianity became the religion of the West, with millions of adherents, it looked as though Jesus had beaten the competition, that is, the competition of Moses and his followers. The "Moses with horns" had been replaced by the "Christ with horns."

But not so fast. The followers of Moses continued to worship and keep the law and maintain their faithful witness. True, Christians outnumbered Jews, and, yes, Christianity did become the state religion of the West. And then, alas, Jews suffered tragic discrimination and persecution at the hands of so-called Christian nations, culminating in the demonic activity of the Nazi regime in the Holocaust.

However, in popular Christian thinking, Jesus appeared to have beaten out the competition with over a billion disciples compared to a few million disciples of Moses. But don't be so sure, says Paul. It is God's intent to save Moses' people every bit as much as it is his intent to save Jesus' people. And while traditional Christianity has suggested its covenant with God superseded the Mosaic covenant, don't be so sure, says Paul and many contemporary writers. The witness of Moses' people in the world is powerful and pervasive, exemplary and enduring.

Jesus is doing okay with the competition of Moses. But we need to remember that in the Transfiguration vision they both were God's men, talking *with* one another about their continuing work.

II

How is Jesus doing with the competition? Let's turn from the lawgiver Moses to *the prophet Elijah.* How is Jesus doing with the prophets? If Matthew's Gospel portrays Jesus as a new Moses or lawgiver, Mark and Luke portray him as a new Elijah or prophet. If the ninth century B.C. Elijah was to reappear to prepare the way for the Messiah, John the Baptist was that Elijah. But now, say the Gospels, someone greater than a prophet is here, namely Jesus, the beloved Son of God, the transfigured, radiant one.

Jesus was indeed one who stood in the tradition of the prophets. Like Amos and Jeremiah before him, he was critical of those focused on the ritual of Temple worship to the neglect of ethics and good deeds. He would agree with Micah and Isaiah that the practice of justice is better than sacrifice, and the doing of righteousness better than burned offerings. If the priests were devoted to the legalistic rituals of altar and sanctuary, Jesus was devoted to the humanistic deeds of compassion in the streets and marketplace.

And while the great prophets Elijah, Amos, Isaiah, and Jeremiah hold an exalted position in our minds and hearts, Jesus holds an even higher position. He's doing well with the competition, and, of course, in traditional Christian thinking, supersedes the competition. Yet, it is to be noted that in the transfiguration vision, Jesus and Elijah are talking *with* one another. They are on the same team.

However, a new and powerful prophet has appeared on the scene by the name of Mohammed. Born in Arabia in 570 A.D., and dying in 632 A.D., the religion Mohammed founded now has at least three-quarters of a billion adherents throughout the world. "Allah is most great and Mohammed is his prophet," chant millions of Muslims worldwide. The word *Islam* means "submission," and perhaps that submission is never more graphically expressed than seeing thousands of Muslims prostrate themselves five times a day

149

in devout prayer. "Allah is great and Mohammed is his prophet," they chant. And in many quarters, the Koran, Mohammed's book, is completely memorized by devout believers.

Mohammed never denied the divine revelation accorded to Judaism and Christianity. Indeed, Jesus himself is often mentioned in the Koran. Mary, Jesus' mother, is mentioned twice as many times in the Koran as in the New Testament. Jesus' virgin birth is affirmed. The Koran says that only Adam's and Jesus' souls were directly created by God. Jesus is regarded as a greater wonder-worker than Mohammed. And while the Koran denies the cruci-fixion and resurrection of Jesus, it nonetheless affirms his Second Coming. And to this day when Muslims say the name Jesus, they add, "May peace be upon him."

So as a prophet, Mohammed is doing very well in competition with Jesus. At least three-quarters of a billion people revere Mohammed as God's last and final and superior prophet. But alas, zealous followers of Mohammed have been all too willing to kill followers of Jesus, just as zealous followers of Jesus have been all too willing to kill followers of Moses.

How is Jesus doing with the competition? Perhaps we should consider expanding the Transfiguration vision to show Jesus talk-ing not only with Moses and Elijah, but also with Mohammed and Mohammed with them. Could it be that Almighty God is continu-ing his work through all three? Should we, as some Muslims ad-vocate, begin talking about the Judeo-Christian-Muslim tradition?

It has been said that some of the bloodiest wars of history have been religious wars, wars fought in the name of Jehovah or God or Allah. That is surely true, even though equally bloody wars have been fought over oil, gold, land, power, and women. Yet, would it not please God if Judaism, Christianity, and Islam — the monothe-istic, Abrahamic religions — began to think of themselves as be-ing on the same side, on the same team, devoted to the same God? Perhaps it's a matter not so much of competition as cooperation where possible, and compatibility against the larger foes of igno-rance, poverty, oppression, evil, and injustice.

III

But of course, there are some other significant world religious leaders missing in this Transfiguration vision. We Christians have been accustomed to looking and seeing only the glory of Jesus. But increasingly in our pluralistic world, we are seeing not only Jesus, but Moses, Elijah, Mohammed, and then a Hindu guru, Buddha, and Confucius. In a world shrunk by travel, trade, communication, and education, pluralism presses in upon us and the Mount of Transfiguration becomes crowded with several holy men of radiance and glory. What should Christians do amid all the competition?

Renowned expert on world religions Huston Smith says that we ought to give up the notion that one religion is superior to another. He agrees with historian Arnold Toynbee that no one alive "knows enough to say with confidence whether one religion is superior to the others ..." (*The World's Religions*, p. 385).

But equally wrong, says Smith, is a reductionism of saying all religions are basically the same. Some will claim that we all have a version of the Golden Rule, and that we all believe more or less in something, and pray, in some form or other, and at least direct our prayers like some Unitarians "to whom it may concern"! The truth is, each religion has distinctive characteristics which are as tenacious and enduring as Christian denominationalism. Most of us don't mind all religions being reduced to one so long as they are reduced to our religion!

A third conception Dr. Smith likes is that of the image of light being refracted through a stained glass window. Just as light is broken into various colors, so too the revelation of God is couched in idioms appropriate to its respective hearers in its respective religions, says Dr. Smith. Even the Koran suggests this in Surah 14:4: "We never sent a messenger except with the language of his people, so that he might make (the message) clear for them" (*ibid.* p. 386).

Huston Smith goes on to suggest that in our age of pluralism we should draw upon the wisdom traditions which are implicit and important in most of the major religions. The Ten Commandments sum up a basic code of ethics for all. The world would be a lot better off without murder, thieving, lying, coveting, and adultery.

151

Most all of the religions teach the virtues of humility, charity, and veracity. And the obstacles to achieving them — namely, greed, hatred, and delusion — are emphasized by most religions.

Most major religions also offer a vision of reality wherein things cohere, hold together, and make sense. There is a grand design and behind the grand design is the perfect Being. And this, says Smith, "causes the wisdom traditions to flame with an ontological exuberance that is nowhere else to be found" (*ibid.*, p. 388).

And behind it all is mystery, not a mystery to be solved like a murder mystery, but a mystery which is incomprehensible, enticing us forward to new dimensions of reality. It is like swimming in the ocean — we participate in it, feel its reality and power, but we never comprehend it.

And so the great religions tell us, says Smith, that "things are more integrated than they seem, they are better than they seem, and they are more mysterious than they seem..." (*ibid.*, p. 389). Thus at the center of the religious life is "a particular kind of joy, a prospect of a happy ending that blossoms from necessarily painful beginnings, the promise of human difficulties embraced and overcome" (*ibid.*).

So on this Transfiguration Sunday, perhaps we need to revise the vision of Moses and Elijah and Jesus to add all the other great religious figures, people like Buddha, Confucius, and Mohammed. We'll need to listen to each, to learn from each other, to understand each other, and perhaps who knows — even to love each other.

And if Jesus can lead us to that, then I guess we need Jesus only. And, of course, the Jesus I love has been my principal master teacher, Lord, and Savior. I have been led to God through him and see him as the very wisdom and word of God, as do millions. And with me he has "beat the competition." But in his loving spirit, my guess is that if others are led to the Divine Father by his so-called "competitors," he would in love and humility say, "Let it be so. For that was my mission in the world — to lead all to the Divine Father."

Prayer

Almighty God, mystery of all mysteries, whose mind and power pervade the universe, and whose presence is ever near, yet ever far, we worship and adore you as you draw us out of ourselves toward light and life as the sun draws flowers and trees toward itself. We are fearfully and wonderfully made, riding on the wings of mystery and participating in the uncertainties of time and space. We give thanks and praise for all we have received.

Be pleased to visit us again with a new vision and a deeper understanding of your designs for our lives. Draw us again to the holy mountain where, like your holy men of old, we might be filled with the assurance of your presence and be radiant with the glory of your love. Take away the clouds of ignorance, the mists of conceit and arrogance, the fogs of timidity and fear. Help us behold Moses and Elijah and Jesus again, with all your special messengers revealing your will. In this age of pluralism, help us perceive the primary messages you wish us to see and hear.

We pray this day for all the major religions of the world and their millions of believers. Help us grow in our appreciation of one another and show us how to cooperate in ways that please your divine plan and will. Keep us from fanaticism and zealotry which lead to hatred and war. Cause us all to be confident of your grace and mercy with assurance that our lives have meaning and purpose. Through Jesus Christ our Lord. Amen.

Bibliography

Barrett, William. *Time of Need.* Harper & Row, New York, NY, 1972.

Bork, Robert H. *Slouching Towards Gomorrah.* Regan Books, New York, NY, 1996.

Branscomb, Bennett Harvie. *The Teachings of Jesus.* Abingdon Press, New York, NY, 1931.

Carter, Stephen L. *The Culture of Disbelief.* Basic Books, New York, NY, 1993.

Durant, Will and Ariel. *The Lessons of History.* Simon and Schuster, New York, NY, 1968.

Durant, Will. *Caesar and Christ.* Simon and Schuster, New York, NY, 1944.

Gilder, George. *Wealth and Poverty.* Basic Books, New York, NY, 1981.

Kierkegaard, Soren. *For Self-Examination.* Augsburg Publishing House, Minneapolis, MN, 1940.

May, Rollo. *Love and Will.* W.W. Norton, New York, NY, 1969.

McIver, Robert. *The Ramparts We Guard.* Elliots Books, New York, NY, 1952.

Menninger, Karl. *Whatever Became of Sin?* Hawthorn Books, New York, NY, 1973.

Nash, Ogden. *I Wouldn't Have Missed It.* Little, Brown and Company, Boston, MA, 1975.

Niebuhr, Reinhold. *Love and Justice*. Westminster Press, Philadelphia, PA, 1957.

Niebuhr, Reinhold. *The Children of Light and The Children of Darkness*. Charles Scribner's Sons, New York, NY, 1944.

Peck, M. Scott. *The Road Less Traveled*. Simon and Schuster, New York, NY, 1978.

Shapley, Harlow. *Beyond The Observatory*. Charles Scribner's Sons, New York, NY, 1967.

Siegel, Bernie, *Love. Medicine and Miracles*. Harper & Row, New York, NY, 1986.

Smith, Huston, *The World's Religions*, HarperSanFrancisco, San Francisco, CA, 1991.

The Interpreter's Bible, Volume 1. Abindgon Press, New York, NY, 1952.

Tillich, Paul. *The New Being*. Charles Scribner's Sons, New York, NY, 1955.

Toffler, Alvin. *Future Shock*. Random House, New York, NY, 1970.

Tournier, Paul. *The Meaning of Persons*. Harper & Brothers Publishers, New York, NY, 1957.

Wells, H. G. *The Outline of History*. The Macmillan Company, New York, NY, 1922.